# The Best of Alberta

Illingworth Kerr, *Oblique Fields*, 1949, oil on canvas.

Canola fields, near Red Deer.

# THE BEST OF
# ALBERTA

## Tom Radford & Harry Savage

featuring
the writing of Mark Abley, R. Ross Annett, Edmund Kemper Broadus, Annora Brown,
Lovat Dickson, Bob Edwards, Caterina Edwards, Joy Kogawa, Myrna Kostash, Henry Kreisel,
Robert Kroetsch, W.O. Mitchell, Howard O'Hagan, Judy Schultz, Allan Shute, Wallace Stegner,
Merna Summers, Lewis G. Thomas, Jon Whyte, Rudy Wiebe

and
the art of James Agrell-Smith, Elliot Barnes, Maxwell Bates, Annora Brown, Ihor Dmytruk,
H.G. Glyde, Nicholas de Grandmaison, Byron Harmon, Carole Harmon, Alex Janvier,
Illingworth Kerr, A.C. Leighton, Barbara Leighton, Pat McCormick, Harold McCrea,
Don McVeigh, Janet Mitchell, Marion Nicoll, William Panko, W.J. Phillips, Winold Reiss,
Clifford Robinson, Carl Rungius, Roy Salopree, Robert Scott, Orest Semchishen, Margaret Shelton,
Wendy Toogood, Sylvain Voyer, Joe Weiss

Hurtig Publishers

Edmonton

Hurtig Publishers Ltd.
10560 - 105 Street
Edmonton, Alberta
Canada  T5H 2W7

**Canadian Cataloguing in Publication Data**

Main entry under title:
The Best of Alberta

ISBN 0-88830-319-X

1. Canadian literature (English) - Alberta.
2. Alberta in literature. 3. Alberta in art.
4. Alberta - Description and travel - Views.
I. Radford, Tom, 1946-      II. Savage, Harry.
  PS8255.A4B48 1987  C813'.54  C87-091316-6
  PR9193.R23 1987

Typesetting by Pièce de Résistance
Design: BOOKENDS DESIGNWORKS/Bob Young
Printed and bound in Canada

TEXT CREDITS

Mark Abley, *Beyond Forget, Rediscovering
  the Prairies*, pp. 195-204. (Vancouver:
  Douglas & McIntyre, 1986)
R. Ross Annett, "It's Gotta Rain
  Sometime", *Especially Babe*, pp. 17-30.
  (Edmonton: Tree Frog Press, 1978)
Edmund Kemper Broadus, *Saturday and
  Sunday*. (Toronto: Macmillan)
Annora Brown, *Annora Brown/Sketches
  from Life*. (Edmonton, Hurtig, 1981)
Lovat Dickson, *The Ante-Room*,
  pp. 219-227. (Toronto: Totem, 1975)
  Reprinted with the permission of
  Johnathan Lovat Dickson.
Bob Edwards, *The Best of Bob Edwards*,
  edited by Hugh A. Dempsey.
  (Edmonton: Hurtig, 1975)
Joy Kogawa, *Obasan*, pp. 1-4. (Toronto:
  Lester and Orpen Dennys, 1981)
Henry Kreisel, "The Travelling Nude",
  from *The Almost Meeting and Other
  Stories*, pp. 1-17. Reprinted with
  permission of NeWest Publishers Ltd.
  (Edmonton: NeWest, 1981)
Myrna Kostash, *All of Baba's Children*,
  pp. 171-180. (First published in
  Edmonton: Hurtig, 1980; second
  edition, Edmonton: NeWest, 1987)
Robert Kroetsch, *Badlands*, pp. 138-145.
  (Toronto: General, 1981)
W.O. Mitchell, *The Vanishing Point*,
  pp. 45-54. (Toronto: Seal Books, 1983)
Howard O'Hagan, "The White Horse",
  from *More Stories from Western
  Canada*, edited by Rudy Wiebe and
  Aritha van Herk, pp. 1-12 (Toronto:
  Macmillan, 1980)
Judy Schultz, *Nibbles and Feasts*,
  pp. 37-38. Reprinted courtesy Tree Frog
Press. (Edmonton: Tree Frog Press, 1986)
Allan Shute, *The Riverdale Gazette*
  (Edmonton: Tree Frog Press)
Wallace Stegner, excerpt from *Wolf
  Willow*, pp. 6-8. ©1962 by Wallace
  Stegner. Reprinted by permission of
  Macmillan of Canada, a division of
  Canada Publishing Corporation
Merna Summers, "The Skating Party",
  *West of Fiction*, edited by Leah Flater,
  Aritha van Herk, and Rudy Wiebe.
  (Edmonton, NeWest Publishers, 1983)
Jon Whyte, *WJP* (Edmonton, Longspoon
  Press, 1981)
Rudy Wiebe, *The Temptations of Big
  Bear*, pp. 405-415. (Toronto: McClelland
  and Stewart, 1973)

PHOTO CREDITS

All photographs by Harry Savage except:
Orest Semchishen p. 115 to p. 125;
Tom Radford pp. 20, 41, 52, 63, 109(2),
133, 138, 142, 164, 165, 169(2), 209;
Lauren Dale pp. 25, 81, 127, 141, 220;
Pat McCormick (Provincial Museum of
Alberta) pp. 40, 49(4); Douglas Udell pp.
93, 213; Elliot Barnes (tinting by Carole
Harmon) p. 171; Michael Burns p. 100;
Eddie Klopenstein p. 16; Mike Pinder
(The Edmonton Journal) p. 96; Jerry
Blitzstein p. 65

ACKNOWLEDGEMENTS

The authors would like to express their
appreciation to the following people and
organizations for their help in preparing
this volume:
  Alberta Art Foundation
  Marie Atymichuck
  Doug Barry
  Edward Cavell
  Norine Coad
  Jim Davies
  Roger Deegan
  Mary Dover
  Edmonton Art Gallery
  Bruno Engler
  Al Forbes
  Glenbow Museum
  Jack Gorman
  Harlan Greene
  Audrey Greenough
  Gwyneth & Fred Kelson
  Katherine Lippset
  Pat McCormick
  Roylene Morton
  W.T. Ng
  Arthur Patterson
  Joan & Art Pedlar
  Mary Porter
  Nick Porter
  Eva Radford
  Naomi Radford
  Elizabeth Savage
  Peter & Shirley Savage
  Ena Schneider
  Allan Shute
  Maeve Spain
  Tom, David, & Doris Usher
  Sylvia Vance
  Marylu Walters
  Whyte Museum of the Canadian Rockies

# CONTENTS

For Eva and Elizabeth

# Introduction
## A Sense of Place

Suddenly the male eagle hunched himself and launched forth into space. The air rushed coldly at him as he beat his way into a current that followed up a ravine. Then he set his great tawny wings against it and let the draught carry him aloft, swinging in great arcs. His mate followed, and their spiral ascent took them high above the valley, till it became a flat pattern of white and blue and brown winding snake-like over the prairies, and the prairies had only substance in pin-prick fence posts, match-like telephone poles, scrambled dots of farm buildings, and specks of livestock huddling in the lee of straw-stacks. Fifty miles away, beyond the foothills, the Rockies cragged up in snow-capped purple glory.

This was the eagle's marvellous world. . . .

The writer is a painter, Illingworth Kerr, and the "marvellous world" is Alberta. He was writing in 1939 for an English periodical, *Blackwoods Magazine*, describing the foothills he wandered as a young farm hand and trapper who loved to observe and draw animals. Today at 82 he still paints the Alberta landscape with the energy and daring of a man one third his age. Two of his paintings, "Oblique Fields" and "March Night Foothills", open this book.

Kerr has seen the west with a native's eye, his experience of the country sure and deep. Born in the Qu'Appelle Valley of Saskatchewan, where local merchants gave him his start as a sign painter, he later studied with the Group of Seven in Toronto, lived for a time in England and France and on Canada's west coast before deciding in 1947 to make his home in Alberta. For twenty years he was a teacher and head of what became the Alberta College of Art, but his calling was always that of a painter. He has come back to the same area south of Calgary year after year, searching out the ever-changing texture and light of the valleys and foothills that stretch away from the eastern slope of the Rocky Mountains. Mixing the colours of his palette — the smoky pinks and blues of distant horizons, the cadmium yellow and viridian green of spring fields — Kerr brings to life an Alberta we too often take for granted.

The day we photographed him at work near Millarville, Kerr was befriended by Frank Sharp, an unassuming old cowboy, who turned out to be 1926 World's Champion All Round Bareback Rider. Sharp was just driving around visiting neighbours in a beat-up half-ton truck when he came upon this odd looking gentleman fencing with his paintbrush. Maybe it was the day itself — late October, clear as a bell, two days of fresh snow on the Rockies yet warm enough to take your coat off — but they got to talking: the Calgary Stampede as it used to be, getting busted up riding in Madison Square Garden, oldtimers, newcomers, good neighbours, bad neighbours, the boom, the bust. "You don't paint that god-damned modern art do you?" Two complete strangers, two utterly different worlds, yet they had time for each other, and between them you could sense something we like to think of as Albertan. Edward Chapman, a little known and overblown Victorian poet described it this way:

Out where the hand clasp's a little stronger
Out where the smile lasts a little longer
That's where the West begins.

This is the country Princess Louise Caroline Alberta, fourth daughter of Queen Victoria, would have encountered when she accompanied her husband, the Marquess of Lorne, Canada's Governor General from 1878-1883, on his tour of the then North West Territories. It is after this elegant lady that the province is named.

Princess Louise Caroline Alberta.

Eastern slope of the Rockies from the Porcupine Hills. Their Blackfoot name, *ky-es-kaghp-ogh-suy-iss*, means porcupine tail. Palliser referred to the area as Montagne de Porquepique when he mapped the region.

Kerr soon returned to his painting and we proceeded down the road to a dead end, and down a cart path that winds through fields of tall grain to "Cottonwoods", the stock farm of Gwynydd Kelson. The white frame house, the barn, and out-buildings are spread out along the banks of Sheep Creek, within view of its source in the Rockies. In summer the Cottonwoods garden abounds with the bloom of delphiniums, monkshood, white daisies, hollyhocks and larkspur, flowers grown yearly from the successors of the hardy seeds her parents and neighbours brought from across continents and oceans to soften life in a strange and hostile environment.

Her brother, Lewis Gwynne Thomas, professor emeritus of history at the University of Alberta and author of "Gardening in Alberta", which appears in this book, grew up with her here. He now lives at Kapasiwin, west of Edmonton, on Lake Wabamun, but each year an exchange of seeds and cuttings makes its way back and forth between their two gardens, keeping alive a treasured aspect of the history of a family.

For over a century now, throughout the province an ever-increasing array of gardens has burst into bloom every spring, accompanied by the warmth of a returning sun, the scent of freshly turned earth. A five-minute drive from Cottonwoods, the Millarville flower show annually brings together the local community of farmers, ranchers, and townspeople that Lewis Thomas grew up with. As in the best of Kerr's paintings, a strong sense of place underlies the day's events — the strawberry tea with its freshly baked scones, cream, and berries in the Christ Church parish hall; the quiet conversation; the deep-seated values and traditions of country life. From the surrounding hills you can see the towers of Calgary on the distant horizon, but they seem a century away.

Some 400 miles to the north and east lies a rolling parkland of field and forest, home to a scattering of farming communities built at the turn of the century. Bruderheim — the German "home of the brothers"; Myrnam — Ukrainian for "peace to us"; Thorhild — in honour of the Norwegian god of thunder; Innisfree — after "the bee loud glades" of Ireland. Myrna Kostash, an Edmonton writer, returns to this country every spring, to a farm near Two Hills she has named "Tulova," after the Galician village her ancestors left behind in what is now the Soviet Union. She wrote of it in *The Camrose Review*:

April. I open the shaky cabin door and the cold air, trapped during the winter, meets me. I stand in the doorway. I see myself at the desk, looking out the east-facing window towards the soil that rolls to the North Saskatchewan. I see myself in the big green armchair, reading from the light of the kerosene lamp. I see myself lighting this lamp and walking about barefoot in the long white nightgown, empress of a single room.

I walk into the room and push open the draughty windows. They frame the still-lifeless trees; thus framed they are as I last looked at them, through this glass in October. The grasses round the cabin are sere and yellow and dusty. If there are birds, they are hiding. This little world is very still, not even the wind is breathing. We are all waiting, holding our breath, as though we do not believe that it will ever be hot again. . . .

I have a right to be here. This cabin with its lands are my inheritance, bequeathed by the generation in the boneyards a few miles away. I name the dead again, pointing out the half-effaced Cyrillic letters on their eroding tombstones. I scrabble in the dirt, remarking the boundaries of their settler's effort: this far and no further into the bush. From one of their villages I have taken a name and nailed it to the wall outside the door.

It is spring and I am ready to live here again."

Kostash's best known work, *All of Baba's Children*, excerpted later in this book, chronicles the lives of the Ukrainian women and men who settled the area, bringing a strong social and political flavour to the province's life. She is very much a modern writer yet her sense of place is also to be found here in the hand-painted interiors of Byzantine churches, visions of an ancient, mystical world transplanted to this northern landscape. A great deal of our culture can be traced to these great leaps of faith — the immigrants' dreams of a new country — yet for Kostash the injustices, the humiliations, the intolerance heaped upon a minority culture must also be remembered. As deep as her feelings for this country may be, they are rooted as much in anger as in the romance of a frontier society. Her Alberta has an edge to it, a residing suspicion of mainstream culture and its power to homogenize or obliterate the details of life.

Yet this day the return of a prairie spring ties her to a Gwynydd Kelson, an Illingworth Kerr, a Lewis Thomas. A land coming back to life; once again full of new prospects, the sense of place confirmed.

Margaret Shelton, *Second Falls, Johnson's Canyon*, 1984, linocut in five colours.

Edmund Broadus, one of Lewis Thomas' teachers at the University of Alberta summed up the sentiment in an essay he wrote in 1909 when he arrived in Edmonton.

... the key to this new life lay in the fact that it was at the end of the line. Everywhere in the day's work and in the day's play, at the desk, in the shop, in the counting-house, on the farm, one felt the underlying consciousness that routine, tradition, the treadmill of blind habit, lay back there in a country where the rails had already passed. Back there, life was an accomplished fact, a finished machine into which you must be content to fit as a cog into its groove. But here life was in the making, still to be hammered into shape and use. And you were not merely a cog. Instead you wielded the hammer. And so you bared your arms with the feeling that you were in at the making of life, and that, in the casting off of the old and the shaping of the new, you had found yourself.

He was about to become a westerner.

*Tom Radford, Harry Savage*
*March, 1987.*

# CHINOOK

Illingworth Kerr, *March Night Foothills*, 1979, acrylic on canvas.

Torrington.

*Opposite:*
Farm west of Millarville.

Cattle grazing along the foothills, near Longview.

Prairie Anemone, Pine Lake.

Calypso Orchid near Jasper.

Viper's Bugloss, along the shore of the Crowsnest River.

The Mountain Bluebird, in spite of its name, is as common to the grasslands as to the alpine regions of the province.

Shooting Stars, near Tees.

*Opposite:*
Rappelling on Mount Sorrow. Angel Glacier and Mount Edith Cavell in the background.

Spring barley, west of Rumsey, one of the early Jewish farming settlements in the province.

*Parnassius smintheus* butterfly near Crowsnest Mountain.

Lac La Biche Fish Derby. The region is famous for its fishing. In nearby Seibert Lake trophy pike weigh 35 lbs.

White Pelicans near Heinsburg.

Looking into the Hand Hills, above Delia.

St. Stephen's Church, near Police Outpost Provincial Park.

# ROOTS

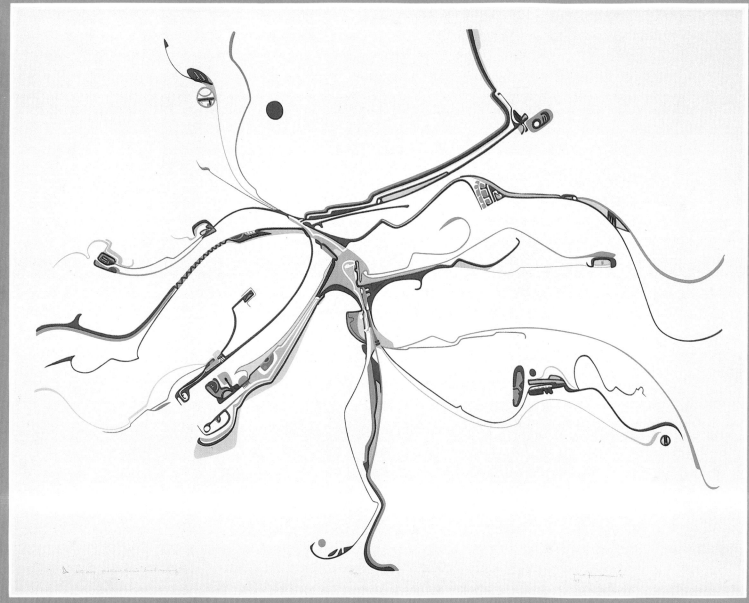

Alex Janvier, *Shallow Praise, Good Morning*, 1975, serigraph.

Early morning, east of Berwyn, overlooking the valley of the Peace.

# Excerpt from *OBASAN*

## by
## Joy Kogawa

*9:05 p.m. August 9, 1972.*

The coulee is so still right now that if a match were to be lit, the flame would not waver. The tall grasses stand without quivering. The tops flop this way and that. The whole dark sky is bright with stars and only the new moon moves.

We come here once every year around this time, Uncle and I. This spot is half a mile from the Barkers' farm and seven miles from the village of Granton where we finally moved in 1951.

"Nothing changes ne," I say as we walk towards the rise.

"Umi no yo," Uncle says, pointing to the grass. "It's like the sea."

The hill surface, as if responding to a command from Uncle's outstretched hand, undulates suddenly in a breeze, with ripple after ripple of grass shadows, rhythmical as ocean waves. We wade through the dry surf, the flecks of grass hitting us like spray. Uncle walks jerkily as a baby on the unsure ground, his feet widespread, his arms suddenly out like a tightrope walker's when he loses his balance.

"Dizzy?" I ask, grabbing him as he wobbles unsteadily on one leg.

His lips make small smacking sounds as he sucks in air.

"Too much old man," he says and totters back upright.

When we come to the top of the slope, we find the dip in the ground where he usually rests. He casts around to make sure there are no wild cactus plants, then slowly folds down onto his haunches, his root-like fingers poking the grass flat in front of him.

Below us the muddy river sludges along its crooked bed. He squats and I stand in the starlight, chewing on bits of grass. This is the closest Uncle ever gets to the ocean.

"Umi no yo," he always says.

Everything in front of us is virgin land. From the beginning of time, the grass along this stretch of prairie has not been cut. About a mile east is a spot which was once an Indian buffalo jump, a high steep cliff where the buffalo were stampeded and fell to their deaths. All the bones are still there, some sticking right out of the side of a fresh landslide.

Uncle could be Chief Sitting Bull squatting here. He has the same prairie-baked skin, the deep brown furrows like dry river beds creasing his cheeks. All he needs is a feather headdress, and he would be perfect for a picture postcard — "Indian Chief from Canadian Prairie" — souvenir of Alberta, made in Japan.

Some of the Native children I've had in my classes over the years could almost pass for Japanese, and vice versa. There's something in the animal-like shyness I recognize in the dark eyes. A quickness to look away. I remember, when I was a child in Slocan, seeing the same swift flick-of-a-cat's-tail look in the eyes of my friends.

The first time Uncle and I came here for a walk was in 1954, in August, two months after Aunt Emily's initial visit to Granton. For weeks after she left, Uncle seemed distressed, pacing back and forth, his hand patting the back of his head. Then one evening, we came here.

It was a quiet twilight evening, much like tonight. His agitation seemed to abate as we walked through the waving grass, though his eyes still stabbed at the air around him and occasionally at me.

When we reached the edge of the hill, we stopped and looked down at the coulee bottom and the river with the tree clumps and brush along its edge. I felt apprehensive about rattlesnakes and wanted to get back to the road.

"Isn't it dangerous?" I asked.

Uncle is almost never direct in his replies. I felt he was chiding me for being childishly afraid when he said abruptly, "Mo ikutsu? What is your age now?"

"Eighteen," I said.

He shook his head as he scuffed the ground. He sighed so deeply that when he exhaled, his breath was a groan.

"What is the matter, Uncle?"

He bent down and patted the grass flat with his hands, shaking his head slowly. "Too young," he said softly. "Still too young." He smiled the gentle half-sad, half-polite smile he reserves for small children and babies. "Some day," he said.

Whatever he was intending to tell me "some day" has not yet been told. I sometimes wonder if he realizes my age at all. At thirty-six, I'm hardly a child.

I sit beside him in the cool of this patch of prairie and immediately I am hidden with him in a grass forest. My hands rest beside his on the knotted mat of roots covering the dry earth, the hard untilled soil.

"Uncle," I whisper, "why do we come here every year?"

He does not respond. From both Obasan and Uncle I have learned that speech often hides like an animal in a storm.

My fingers tunnel through a tangle of roots till the grass stands up from my knuckles, making it seem that my fingers are the

Lily pond, Calgary.

Nikka Yuko Japanese Gardens, Lethbridge. The buildings and bridges were built in 1967 in Japan and re-assembled in Lethbridge. They are gardens of contemplation built around an intricate design of water, rocks, and shrubs.

roots. I am part of this small forest. Like the grass, I search the earth and the sky with a thin but persistent thirst.

"Why, Uncle?"

He seems about to say something, his mouth open as he stares straight ahead, his eyes wide. Then, as if to erase his thoughts, he rubs his hands vigorously over his face and shakes his head.

Above and around us, unimaginably vast and unbroken by silhouette of tree or house or any hint of human handiwork, is the prairie sky. In all my years in Southern Alberta, I have not been able to look for long at this. We sit forever, it seems, in infinite night while all around us the tall prairie grasses move and grow, bending imperceptibly to the moon's faint light.

Finally, I touch his arm. "Wait here awhile," I say as I stand up and walk to the edge of the hill. I always pick at least one flower before we go home. I inch my way down the steep path and along the stretch where the side of the slope oozes wet from the surface seepage of the underground stream. Wild rose bushes, prickly and profuse with green, cluster along the edges of the trickle. I can smell them as I descend. At the bottom of the coulee I can hear the gurgling of the slowly moving water. I stand for a long time watching as the contours of the coulee erode slowly in the night.

# Excerpt from
## *ALL OF BABA'S CHILDREN*

by
Myrna Kostash

The culture that the Ukrainian immigrants brought with them from Europe was an agrarian and almost tribal culture. It was indigenous to the Ukraine, the upper classes having long before adopted, chameleon-like, the styles of whatever imperial state was ruling the country at the time. The customs of a villager in Galicia would have been as "quaint" to a burgher in Lviv as to an Austrian field-marshall. Of course, at the time they brought their culture over to Canada, it didn't occur to the immigrants that this was a Ukrainian or national culture; it was simply the way they lived the daily round of life at home and since they had never travelled even ten miles away they had no way of knowing that they shared common modes of cultural expression with thousands of others. Even in Canada, where people from the same community tended to settle together and even to name the new towns after their old country birthplaces, they did not necessarily see themselves as members of a "nation." This identity would develop in response to the propaganda work of the intelligentsia who, through reading and political work, did understand that Bukovynians and Galicians and Hutzuls were all scattered tribes of a formerly integrated nation-state — Ukraine — and that the folkways of the peasants were the remnants of a mass culture. This national identity would also become much more self-conscious among the first generation who did travel about Canada and who learned that children of people from Snyatyn (in southern Galicia) were raised with very much the same set of cultural habits as the children of people from Sokal (in northwestern Galicia).

But from the very first day of settlement the Ukrainian folk culture began evolving as a Ukrainian-Canadian one. In the first place, the material conditions of life in Europe could not be reproduced exactly in Canada and so cultural forms altered accordingly. Leisure time was drastically reduced: when they had to clear bush and plow virgin soil there was little time for embroidering pillow cases and rehearsing plays. The variety of tools and fabrics and dyes and instruments were not immediately available so they made do with what they had — a crude handloom, coarse hemp, dye from saskatoon berries, a Jew's harp — and created arts and crafts that were not only simpler and coarser but also different. The support structure for cultural expression — the churches, the village common, the collective get-togethers — could not be erected immediately and so artistic expression became localized and reduced to essentials: there was only so much music, dance, cooking and sewing that one family could produce. "We learned the Ukrainian carols which we sang at home and when we got bigger we all went carolling. Mom passed along things like embroidery and egg-painting and cooking to the girls. We had holubtsi every Sunday, with fresh homemade bread."

In addition, the Ukrainian culture in Canada was a minority culture, an enclave of peculiarities in a vastness of Anglo-Saxon generality, and it was an inevitable and irreversible pressure that the majority culture brought to bear on the immigrants. The first instinct was to enclose oneself within the familiar forms of Ukrainianness as the "sole means of consolation in the struggle for existence." Once settlement and capital accumulation were secured, once a modicum of English was learned and the children were passing through school, once Ukrainian-Canadians started congregating in towns and encountered Anglo-Saxon values, the second instinct was to open up to the brave, new, flashy, comfortable and desirable world of the Canadian middle-class. When the radio was grafted onto the Ukrainian Christmas carol, the foxtrot onto the *kolomeyka* and Campbell's soup onto *borshch*, the Ukrainian-Canadian culture came of age.

When the first generation was growing up, their culture was "a little bit of this, a little bit of that": an icon and a calendar picture of a blonde "Miss Alberta Wheat Pool" cuddling chicks; bits of embroidery and some eggs dyed simply in one bright colour; a checkered tablecloth and a chocolate Easter bunny; the spinning wheel and Eaton's catalogue; a brilliantly-coloured, hand-loomed bench cover and a Hudson's Bay blanket, grey and black; garlic in the frying pan and a can of Empress strawberry jam on the pantry shelf. Teacher said Christmas was December 25 and there was a school Christmas concert December 22; Mom and Dad said Christmas was January 6, and so you went to church and then ate like a pig.

There were, nevertheless, certain irreducible elements of the original culture that were practiced for at least one more generation. In 1931, an *Alberta Farmer* reporter located, among the Ukrainian-Canadians, spinning wheels ("It seems strange to see the distaff and spindle in the hands of women who find the power washer a great convenience and who send their sons to university"), looms, tapestries, cross-stitch embroidery, quilting, rug-hooking and wood carving. The tapestries had been woven by mothers and grandmothers "unconsciously seeking to escape from the dull imprisonment of routine"; the daughters didn't know how to weave. "The Ukrainian women

Homestead, south of Tulliby Lake, near the Alberta-Saskatchewan border.

no longer gather plants, barks and mosses to make their dyes. They find they can procure the colours they want by using commercial dyes — and who can blame them for lightening their labours. . . ?" "The old Ukrainian embroidery is almost solid; the more modern has a lighter effect," reflecting the lowered priority of embroidery in the allotment of labour time. Cotton bedspreads replace the woven "and that counts when the family washing has to be done by woman power." Concessions made to technology and the changing attitudes to what in fact constituted "recreation". Use a sewing machine and get the job done fast.

The decorated Easter egg, unlike other crafts, had no functional use. It was a decorative object and, for as long as Ukrainian-Canadians cared about such things, it was a domestic symbol of Easter, spring and rebirth; a pre-Christian symbol in fact, celebrating a sun cult (hence the motifs of the spiral, swastika, stars and sunflowers) onto which Christian motifs were ultimately grafted: the cross, the Virgin's tears, the outline of a church. The fact that decorated eggs can be traced back to the Trypillian culture of Neolithic Ukraine may be of interest to ethnologists and archaeologists. The legend of the three Marys who bribed the guards at Christ's grave with decorated eggs may have been known to some of the immigrants. But for the vast majority of Ukrainians in Canada, the preparation of coloured or designed eggs was simply an essential (though unexplained) part of celebrating Easter: they had to have some in the food basket they took to church to be blessed and they had to have them on hand to give out to visitors. If they had the time, the tools and a good eye, they could design marvels of geometry and colour. If they didn't, they just soaked them in a bright dye and ate them for breakfast. It was the thought that counted. The next generation, bereft of the psychology and spiritual culture of the peasant, would enshrine the egg behind glass in a wood frame, the *pysanka*, as objet d'art; the exquisite ones would be the work of leisured women whose mothers had never managed more than two or three colours, a line here, a line there and a squiggle all around.

Mother taught us girls how to decorate Easter eggs. She didn't make them too fancy, just very simple. As long as there was a line around and some leaf. You see, they believed very much in all that from the old country. The line that encircles the egg has no beginning or end so it symbolizes eternity. And a pine tree, she always made a pine tree to signify eter-

nal youth and health. She made roosters, eternity and fulfillment of wishes and always a fish for Christianity. Mother never made reindeers, but other people did. They must have come from a different village. The dyes were all from the old country, beautiful dyes.

Of course, there were always a few farm women whose artist's pride was expressed in very refined and painstaking decorating and embroidery (especially for ornamentation in the church). But the majority, bent exhausted under a kerosene lamp with eyes half closed and hands cracked and calloused, could produce only the crudest arts.

Nothing, however, could cramp the celebration of Christmas and Easter. Traditionally, these were the occasions when the need to gather together and have a good time superceded the demands of the land and when the church's authority became more impressive than the state's. It was the same in Canada. The family's wealth was invested in food, its time in ritual observances and its emotional vulnerability in the mass. Even the sceptics, the anti-clerics, the apostates would repeat the ancient gestures: cooking enormous amounts of food, bundling up for the sled-ride to church, inviting carollers into the house for a drink. They did it because they were Ukrainian and knew no other way — until, that is, the kids came home from school prattling about Santa Claus and Easter bunnies. Foolishness, if not blasphemy! Let Miss Jameson at the school celebrate Christmas and Easter as the joyless and over-sensible Anglo-Saxons saw fit. In this house, the holiday mood would be an orgy of food and prayer. Two weeks before Christmas mother would start the baking — the braided breads, the buns, the honey cake — and the kids would set to with a mortar and pestle, pounding poppy seed into mush. The day before Christmas a spruce tree or simply poplar branches would be strung with home-made decorations, nuts wrapped in foil from cigarette packages, paper chains and berries strung together — a Canadian custom — and the traditional sheaf of wheat propped in a corner. Hay, to symbolize the manger, was spread on the floor under the table and under the tablecloth. Then, finally, jubilantly, at the sighting of the first evening star, the family would eat, all twelve customary dishes if they could afford it, cabbage rolls, borsch, cooked wheat with poppy seed, two or three varieties of fish, bread, lentils, thin, sweet pancakes, cakes, till the candle in the *kolach* flared and went out and the neighbours came around to visit. Christmas Day mass was a five-hour affair. One could miss church all year except for this service. Feast and mass were repeated for Epiphany and the kids would make little crosses out of straw and stick them to the window. They stuck to the inch of ice on the inside of the pane. Throughout the season, carollers went from farm to farm, frozen from the sleigh-ride, thawed from whiskey, refrozen on the ice-bound sled. "January 6 would be our Christmas. We never knew there was one on December 25."

The Easter celebration was intensely religious although there was, like Christmas, the bellyful of food. Easter Thursday's mass. Easter Friday's procession around the church at midnight, men carrying an icon of Christ, girls carrying that of the Virgin Mary: three times around the little church with a band of boys playing noise-makers because the church bells could not be rung at Christ's death. Inside, a crown of thorns and a spear are "buried" in a table in front of the altar, on the altar the icon of Christ, kissed by the devout, crawling on their knees. On Sunday morning, this icon would be carried by the priest to the altar — the Resurrection — and the three huge bells in the wooden belfry in the church yard would ring out and mass would be celebrated until two o'clock in the afternoon — "in those days nobody was in a hurry" — usually without benefit of pews or chairs. After mass, the priest would bless the food baskets of the families: a little *babka* (fruit bread) and *paska* (sweet bread), a piece of pork, raw onion, horseradish, pickled beets and, in a little bowl, cream cheese impressed with a cross of cloves. Finally, at home, the feast. Easter Monday's mass and the afternoon's "fertility rituals" when young men visited young women to throw water at them, a modification of the old country custom of actually throwing the girls into creeks and ponds.

Depending on the degree of one's devotion, one could also celebrate Epiphany and Epiphany Eve, Whitsunday, Feast of Jordan, Saints Peter and Paul Day, not to mention secular holidays commemorating various events important to old country patriots and the birthdays of the most honoured Ukrainian writers. Anything, really, to get out from behind the plough and stove and socialize like a civilized human being.

There was nothing quite so sociable as a wedding and to the extent it was exuberant and bawdy, it was more pagan than Christian. The guests laughed and got drunk and the bride cried; it was a reminder that the community's renewal through marriage was paid for by the sorrows of married women.

Ukrainian Cultural Heritage Village, west of Royal Park. The village brings to life many facets of pioneer life in east-central Alberta.

Dancers, Vegreville.

Helen Bluda, Boyle, homesteaded in the Greenpine area in 1931.

My oldest sister's wedding: Saturday night the bride is getting ready. Her bridesmaids came over to visit. (She was married in '26 at sixteen and he was nineteen.) Mother was getting the food ready. Sunday morning they went to church and got married. The bride and groom came home for dinner. Then he went home by himself, the bride remained in her father's house — that was the custom — until the following Sunday when we had the wedding feast, at his home and at ours at the same time. Dancing, dinner and supper. About four in the afternoon the groom comes with his attendants to get the bride who is usually in the house behind the table. She's in her wedding dress again. They take her dowry — quilts, pillows, trunk — and drive over to the groom's place where he was living with his parents. Everybody's waiting for them there and they have a supper and dance. I know that Mom and Dad met them at the gate after the church service with kolachi. The dinner: borsch, holubtsi, nachynka, roast chicken, jellied salads, cakes, cider. Kolachi but no wedding cake like now. Very elaborate with little birds and beautiful big braids.

By the time I got married it was different already. Went to the church in the morning, came back home for a dinner and had a small reception. A band played, a violin, a drum, tsimbaly, they played good dance music — not Ukrainian dancing though — but at my sister's wedding the men danced the arkan and some ladies would sing such sad, meaningful songs about the girl leaving home and not knowing what her life was going to be like. It would make you cry.

We had a small wedding at home at my mother's place. We were married in Mundare, St. Peter's church on the 12th of June. There were three couples getting married. We were all standing in a row, the bridesmaids at the back of them. I wore a white dress and veil. I had my dress made and the veil was bought and I had sort of metallic shoes on. We had made our bouquets of artificial flowers. We didn't have live ones. The groom came to pick us up and the bridesmaids and the best man came and picked me up and we drove to Mundare to church. And back from the wedding to my mother's place for dinner. In the evening we go down to the groom's place. That was sort of an old fashioned way. We didn't get very many presents, not those days. A donation was maybe a dollar or two from a couple. I think I had three presents at our place and maybe three or four over

here at his place. But the rest was in cash. I got a berry bowl, a fruit bowl, towels and a little tablecloth. Usually, in those days the mother of the bride had some stuff ready for the girl. Like the quilt, the pillows, the sheets and pillow cases, towels. The mothers really prepared for the girl. I didn't have a dowry, but I did get two cows later from my mother. They gave me two good milking cows.

Some elements were introduced as conscious adaptations of the "Canadian" way of getting married — the white dress and veil, the wedding cake, the bridesmaids, the confetti — but the overall format was strictly a Ukrainian production, as long as people got married on the farm. By contrast, a wedding in town would have to be indoors, it couldn't last more than a day (people had nine to five jobs) and the parents of the bride would pay the Ladies' Auxiliary to do the cooking that could no longer be done in the small kitchen of a town house. It remained Ukrainian so long as there were still guests who could remember the dances from the native village, remember all the verses to a song, remember the correct sequence of ritual events from the parents' blessing with the presentation of bread and salt to the "kidnapping" of the bride. Once these passed from memory and, more importantly, from significant meaning, the Ukrainian wedding changed character and acquired the "meaning" imprinted by loose cash (lots of presents), the automobile (all the relatives had to be invited), the electric guitar (more bunny-hops and less *kolomeykas*) and the white-collar job (the bride and groom could honeymoon in Banff).

Music and dance. For awhile, these remained spontaneous expressions of feeling and philosophy among illiterate immigrants with few other means of letting each other know what was on their minds. Songs by the railroad gang about cruel bosses; songs by women sewing together about cruel husbands. Songs at dances about romance and songs at weddings about woman's sorrow. Songs at Christmas about Bethlehem and songs at New Year's about good fortune. Lullabies and nonsense songs, *dumy*; songs about Cossacks. Songs from the caravanserai, the peasant uprisings, the anti-Soviet Ukrainian Insurgent Army. Songs from the Bolshevik Revolution and the Spanish Civil War. Songs about the weather, family history, personal misfortune and daydreams. Hymns. This was the music of people who had not yet experienced the separation of music from everyday activity. It was unselfconscious, it was another way of speaking.

St. Vladimir's Ukrainian Greek Orthodox Church.

Some time ago when we were small, no matter where you went there was singing. To your neighbour's, to your aunt's, there'd be singing. Not that they were singing in four voices but they sang the songs they knew. It didn't matter if you had a voice.

With education, however, singing became more of an accomplishment, in fact, a product offered up to a passive audience by a disciplined choir with a monopoly on formal knowledge of music. Enter the musical expert, exeunt the gratuitous improvisations of the people. Intellectuals with a background in music, who could read and write musical notation and were familiar to a degree with the sophisticated forms of opera and chorale and the varieties of church music, became the musical directors of Ukrainian-Canadian communities through the halls. They harnessed the musical energy of the people by organizing choirs, producing concerts, staging operas and rehearsing orchestras. It became important to be talented: to have a rich voice, to be able to sing in harmony with several voices, read music and follow a conductor. In this way, because only a few members of the community at a time could fulfill the demands of the discipline, music became the privileged expression of a small group of specialists and so, by the time of the first generation's maturity, if they knew any Ukrainian songs it was because they had studied them. Or remembered their mothers singing at night, while darning socks. Their songs were as likely to be English-language pop tunes as Cossack lullabies. There were other effects of this professionalization. For the first time, large numbers of rural Ukrainians heard the songs originally composed for the ruling class in the old country, the operas based on Ukrainian literature and the masses written for urban cathedrals. And, for the first time, the songs of the "folk" were transcribed by notation and passed on to singers who might otherwise never have heard them.

So the making of music was gradually transferred from the home to the public gathering place, to the hall, and to the school. In the hall, at least, the audience was assured of being entertained with a music of its own ethnicity, even if it was based on urban tastes; at the school, they were rather treated to the music of the Anglo-Saxon. By popular demand, if the teacher was Ukrainian, the concert became bi-cultural.

At the school where I was teaching, the students had to buy their own mandolins, or maybe somebody's uncle or somebody's aunt had one. Ukrainian music always lent itself to the mandolin. We used to play half and half, you know. We always had to have some Ukrainian songs. So I learned a few Ukrainian pieces, songs from our songbooks, and a Ukrainian folksong, something that would lend itself to an action song.

I told you that I had a couple of very religious families there and they didn't allow their children to play certain pieces. Their boys were learning the violin and could pick up tunes from the radio. So they would come to school and play us a tune; they knew how to play some of these hillbilly pieces. It was just tremendous what they could play, jigs and that. And of course we were learning to play *Whispering Hope* and a few of these nice pieces and the people clapped so hard for this group, you know, it was a group of grade seven and eight boys, and they clapped so hard and these two brothers from this very religious family looked at me with one eye. Encore, I said, an encore! The kids looked at me real hard, and the mother said, "Well, I guess that's all right, they learned it in school."

Ihor Dmytruk, *Relic*, 1967, woodcut.

# THE PEOPLE

Winold Reiss, *Double Steel and Two Cutter*, n.d., drawing.

# Excerpt from
## *THE TEMPTATIONS OF BIG BEAR*

by
Rudy Wiebe

The white mare Little Bad Man had given him was between his legs; he could feel her hide creak shifting over her ribs. Perhaps too big a black stallion had got on her that summer, her belly sagged lower than drying meat on a string and he couldn't see her head, barely her withers in the whining snow. He tried to stretch forward in the lee of her neck, to get his legs completely back against her hide, but they wouldn't lift, wouldn't so much as bend and the wind cut up under whatever it was he wore, furrowing into his spine like a hot knife. The wind had been partly held along the creek between Cutknife and the Eagle Hills, it had been possible there but now on the prairie it seemed to hurl them south; as if the mare no longer had ground under her feet, simply flung between the trees that grew in short clusters everywhere. They hadn't been there when he hunted buffalo and now the wind used them to wait behind and gather itself and slam him with steel doors, hoisting the white mare off her feet into nothing, her hide against his face cold iron and he could not find his breath. They were getting that too, they were at last, and a bell rang.

"The blankets are there, won't you lie down?" He heard that as gentleness, and he could understand words; they were gentle too. And all wrong for he was standing already as he must, groping about for the grey pants he had certainly folded up properly but there seemed to be nothing, no iron bed and it was Horsechild, would he ever forget the face of his last son and his hands on his shoulder, "Will you lie down?"

"The basin — water, I have to —" but this was really Horsechild, yes. And the walls around him pushed out. Logs and his son's eyes held him firmly out of the wind; there was the heater with his feet beside it burning cold as if on fire, and he gathered his words together, holding hard to the strength in the dark eyes holding him. "Forgive me," he said, and he saw his own hands clamped to his son's shoulders, and could feel that too. A shoulder almost too hard for a boy with fourteen such winters. "I can't lie down yet," he said.

So he was sitting on a blanket by the tin heater with a fire so loud inside it could almost be heard above the storm tramping endlessly over the roof. The fire gradually died in his feet he thought, and it was Horsechild kneeling over them, rubbing them, he could see that and he knew there was no one else in the house which was almost as good as a buffalo lodge, though it could not split the storm around it like a buffalo lodge and of course couldn't be moved either. The Magpie wasn't there; she was outside this house, somewhere, wherever it was

she had as much shelter from the storm as she wanted and could run after and he was too ashamed to say a word to his last son who knew that as well as he; to say anything. He watched the boy far away slowly, gently, work on the two poles that were his legs stretched into the distance; the year and a half in those black tunnels had killed his legs, he couldn't sit like a Person now and when he had let them hang over the iron edge of that iron bed and known that, it had come to him that he was getting closer to where he would have to go anyway now that everything he saw everywhere was dying too. And he was almost resigned sometimes, momentarily, sitting like that.

But his son's strong hands warmed him, he could feel his legs again and so he could ride more easily before the wind, the withers of the mare not so much now like a canoe-bow tossed about white water. When the storm grew worse he could walk now and lead her, keeping warm. He had about bent his knees to do that when it came to him there was no cold along his back; that his legs felt so good he could barely feel them and a lightness something like dawn, not howling snow, swam there ahead of him. He rode on, his heart lifting and the mare steadier on her feet and the Tramping Lakes must be there stroked smooth between the round hills and then he was on a ridge, the hills reaching down like the spring green legs of sleeping buffalo, down to the level blue earth, green legs tipped with blacker green hoofs under bright sky quite empty of sun. He rode down there, heat loosening his frozen face and the mare already quick, her head nodding, swinging easily down and he was among the submerged, inverted trees dipped in buds like yellow syrup and saw the green hills across the water between them, the water one sheet of light and swung his leg over the grey mare's withers and knew it before his feet touched the ground. The thunder of *mustoos-wuk* running the earth. At last, again; here. He stood feeling it, motionlessly listening. They were there, coming, the bulls bellowing in happiness as they ran side by side and the spring calves by their mothers and the dust of their numberless hooves roiled up wherever the horizon would reach and his body was with them a living wand thrust into the earth, shivering to the drum-roll of the charge coming to trample him into itself. He knew, immensely, that whole thunder his thunder and from him burst the roar of the one giant bear that could smash those lunging hindquarters with its swinging paw, rear up and roar with its arms stretched open wide, jaws agape and clamp into

Saddle Lake Pow Wow on the occasion of the community's centennial. Over 300 dancers from across the Canadian and American west were in attendance.

that arched neck, heave and tear the crushed body behind those daggered horns, and through his roars, echo upon echo to the prairie's thunder, slid the thin steel of a tinkling bell.

"I think she heard that at Little Pine's," Horsechild said. "Will you lie down now?" But the bell kept on ringing, a sound so tiny that no sound he would ever make could stop it if it did not wish to stop by itself and he knew by now it would never do that. Finally he said to the endless tall white men all black around him, the tall warden with his black beard and the round black hat that covered his white hair, and all the black robes clustered blacker than so many judges and with tight white collars holding their heads stiffer than any judge, Tâche with the huge silver crosses and Lacombe with his snowy hair wiped back from the glistening dome of his head and all the others craned over him while the bell rang. "Yes," he said finally, "I know now it's what you tell me, Poundmaker was with his father Crowfoot and there he has choked. He died too because he had no breath. I know. You, you can do that to me now if you want."

The bell rang immediately and water was sprinkling upon his head; he could barely feel that as he faced the black toes just sticking out under the edge of black dress scuffed dusty and singing above him with the sharp smell of something burning far up in the gloomy rafters and he lifted his head to the sounding face melting slightly above him, almost discernible, and told it directly just as its eyes hardened and held steady, "Yes, and John McDougall would have a word for People here. I want him to do this too, he'll have that much, that little water left for me too," with the white face soughing into hesitation, its incomprehension melting it like fat and its sound stretching down, down into a long snout of laughter dripping between tiers of teeth. Black fur lifted laughter.

The mare's hide nevertheless was almost glossy white. A song to her strength in the knee-deep grass lifted him riding south, the quick coulees; happiness, he was past the Tramping Lakes and Little Round valley and the sand hill where he had hunted white wolf once too often. The land lay its endless circle around him in distant bluish levels tilting and curving slightly against and over each other; he looked everywhere under the bright sky but there was no sun to be found. The brightness sat like a summer cap and here and there tufts began sticking out of the land almost as if clusters of giant trees sprouted now where wolf willow had barely grown before. He saw then that straight lines had squared up the land at right angles, broad lines of

Hand game, Fort Chipewyan. Pete Arnault practises his sleight-of-hand in this guessing game at a treaty day celebration. The game was banned by white administrators in the north for many years but is now renewing its place in native culture.

*Opposite:*
Fiddlers' contest, Lac La Biche.

Young grass dancer, Saddle Lake.

The grand entrance, Saddle Lake Pow Wow.

Opening ceremonies, Saddle Lake Pow Wow.

stark bleached bones had been spread straight, pressed and flattened into the earth for him to ride over, and sliced into hills as if that broad thong of bone could knuckle them down, those immovable hills. As far as he could see, wherever he looked the world was slit open with unending lines, squares, rectangles, of bone and between the strange trees gleamed straight lines of, he comprehended it suddenly, white buildings. Square inedible mushrooms burst up under poplars overnight; but square. He could not comprehend where he was. He suddenly recognized nothing where he knew he had ridden since he was tied in the cradleboard on his mother's back, where he had run buffalo since he could fork a horse. He was seeing; the apprehension which the settler-clustered land of Manitoba and Winnipeg's square walls and gutted streets had begun drove like nails into the sockets of himself and his place was gone, he knew Earth and Sun which had been his gifts to accept and love and leave to others were gone, all gone. Only Sky remained, overpowering brightness, floating pillars and tufts of cloud, laughing him into the horror of its final irony with no Thunderbird either; no more rain, the land dead with no Thunderbird to revive it, only the wolfish wind to lick dry and hound endlessly until there was none of it left, even dead, there would be — nothing, not even a hold — just nothing. He was hitting the mare, head, ribs, haunches with his legs and arms like unbendable clubs and she stumbled through the brittle grass, grasshoppers spraying, and he beat her staggering across the hard bleached bones, buffalo and People, yes he could see that, eyeholes in parts of skulls upon the scraped hillsides until he felt her breath sawing its last under him but he was on the hills then looking down, it was the South Saskatchewan — The Forks he recognized, unchanged! and he screamed his cry and hammered the mare down the long tilt of hill he knew he could never have walked, her legs braced and reeling as if she were drunk and he laughed aloud down to the crossing where the land whitened and above him stood Bulls' Forehead Hill, flung with snow which the sear grass sprayed about the mare's floundering hoofs. Under the cottonwoods whorled black like snakes, but the mare refused to touch the river ice; stood shuddering. He battered her then as he never had any animal before, the horror of what he had escaped driving him beyond horror until she strained forward her bloody head away from his bloody fists and staggered out, slipping and almost falling but he heaved her to balance again and again with the sheer power of his shoulders, they still

worked as they once had I yo ho, I yo ho, I am here now! and she was almost to the shadow of the hill when water, there is living water still in this river he roared, broke up black out of whiteness and he gave her to it with great happiness that by his final abuse of her she would find such a good, sweet end as she slid silently down the bending ice, under, and vanished, he lying there on the ice as it groaned and watching, his eyes wide open since the bell must ring now, certainly ring.

But it did not. Horsechild was talking to him, the warm softness of the First People, "You have to lie down now. She'll come back when she comes, you have to lie down."

"Yes… yes, I…." standing now for out of the reddish darkness faintly stinking, he was aware of that, coming towards him he saw at last what he had dreaded so long. The hard boots of Little Man, his white child's clothes and stiff black hat, it was clearly Hodson with glass over his snout making two oval reflections where his bulging eyes should have been. And behind him came the procession; six shapes coming relentlessly and he saw them as he had seen long ago, and knew them in their steady pace, their hands tied behind their backs. Miserable Man lifted his great pitted face and his lips were moving for his hands could not, I want to eat and then be shot, not like this, you tell the boss; old Bad Arrow came head down, and behind him Round The Sky, his kind young face staring where sky should have been, somewhere, but Wandering Spirit was a skeleton still asking Mrs. McLean if he could be forgiven, crouched perhaps by a small fire and asking if punishment would last long, asking, asking and Mrs. McLean certain that God always forgave everyone who truly repented of his wrong, he must now repent for what he had done and put all that away but the soldiers, now the white soldiers…. Little Bear's mouth gaped in warcry, his chin jabbing down at the still unhealed scars on his breast as he came in fury but it was his friend Iron Body alone who spoke aloud. He made very calmly, his lean face without any expression whatever, the longest speech of his life, and it seemed begging too: "We will need different shoes. On the white Jesus road it's a long way to the Sand Hills, and for that you should give us good Whiteskin shoes." He stood motionless and staring, unaware that he could no longer breathe, these six River men who had once respected and loved him, with whom he had once thought that something might be possible, that they could all stand together and build something together that was their own, theirs, of the First People, but for which the power,

Cree girl, Saddle Lake.

wherever it was to do those things he had once perhaps dreamed, perhaps impossibly, had never been given him or he had never taken it when it was there or there wasn't any to take or perhaps it would be a hundred years in coming, he had to face that he knew nothing of it now if he had ever known anything of it as he faced those six River men before him, standing where their individual bits of power had brought them pushing individually against massed whites, and not quite standing either for their heads bulged a little crooked to one side, he had eaten meat with their fathers before they were children, slightly swinging there in a row with blood swelling up, their faces bursting out disfigured in the reddish, stinking darkness and he was beating himself with his head and battering the walls and his head with the steel ball and chain for that bell, the bell, bell you have to ring, bell!

Horsechild was wiping his face. For an instant Bull's Forehead Hill leaning down on him was Stony Mountain forcing him

under the stiff men with guns high and pacing endlessly between the barbwire sagebrush along its crest, but it was really Horsechild's hand upon him, the other wiping his face and he could not so much as raise himself under that thin hand's weight, but then he could and lunged up from the blanket beside the stove. After a time, sitting, he had enough air in his chest once more too, with that sick stench gone.

"Tell me again," he could say then, "everything, about the People, still breathing, start with... Poundmaker."

"Crowfoot buried him on the hill above Blackfoot Crossing."

"Ahh. That was where, his mark on the treaty. Crowfoot. And Sitting Bull?"

"They say he's shooting his gun in a tent and Whiteskins pay to see that. With a Buffalo Bill."

"Buffalo, there are none of those now, Dumont?"

"He's in there too, they say, shooting."

"Yes. And Little Poplar, who showed his wide bare ass to soldiers."

"Soldiers shot him outside their camp in Montana. He was sitting on the wrong horse."

Big Bear found he could not so much as throw his head back, leave alone find breath to make a warcry for his sister's son, dead perhaps like a warrior. He whispered, finally, "He always loved many horses. Lone Man—"

"He was riding the wrong horse too, Cowan's horse from Fort Pitt and a policeman saw him in Edmonton. They say he's in... that place...."

"I know that, I saw him," said Big Bear. "They pushed him down that black tunnel, where they push everyone, there's no time, I want to know about Kingbird. And his son, tell me."

Horsechild said very slowly, "You know, Kingbird and his son are in Montana with... his brother and other River People, down there."

"With Little Bad Man, whose name is now Little Bear?"

"Yes, that one."

"What do they eat?"

"They... hunt, in the Bearpaws...."

"There is nothing to hunt in Montana. How does Little Bear feed The People."

"They...."

"What!"

"Live around the towns in winter. They eat what Whiteskins throw away."

Big Bear was able to whisper, after a long time, "He became

a great warrior, that day on Belly River, facing Bloods all bloody."

"But that kept in a clean place," Horsechild said quickly, "it's here. There under the rafter where I put it, it's there, Kingbird gave it to me when he and Sits Green and the boy had to go south and he said Chief's Son's Hand had to — "

"When you see Little Bear, tell him I remembered at the last hunt there, how he said the Bearpaws was the place for People."

He was looking his apology for interrupting, he had to hurry now and he added as soon as he could, "If you want to, you tell Kapay-tow-aysing he's welcome to her. Maybe he can find, where she has kept her softness."

Big Bear said that, and he was going to say something more to his last son silently facing him, waiting for his word; he was going to say something about Chief's Son's Hand, keep that among the People for they have nothing left, and it seemed that he was actually thinking again those long, long thoughts of power and confederation and of his people living as they would wish, not with buffalo for they were gone, but as People still, somehow, the proud First People. But the bundle given him by Great Parent Bear, the songs that had guided him in his long life, where were they all now? Where were they for his son who might have to live a long time yet? There had always been too much, there was too much he could not understand, leave alone know. He had lived some things wrong and some things right and that was what he had lived. It was time now. To lie down; to finish the long prayer to The Only One that was his life and when he had decided that he stood up from beside the black water easily and walked over the river ice, up between the hills, climbed between the folded hillocks through the hollow of blowouts streaked with running snow and steadily, strongly, up the sand hill. On the top he stood erect and slowly turned in the circle of all that had once been given him. Above him the ghost dancers flamed like torn curtains springing fearfully beautiful out of their own vanishing again and again. He cleansed his hands with sweetgrass, its smell sharp as a good woman in his nostrils. Then he said:

"You Only Great Spirit, Father. I thank you. I thank you for giving me life, for giving me everything, for being still here now that my teeth are gone. So now I have to ask you this last thing, and I think it's like the first thing I asked but maybe you'll forgive that, since you have already known for a long time how hard it is for me to understand and learn anything,

even in all the time you gave me. I ask you again. Have pity."

After these words he was going to lie down immediately but then he felt a warm weight against his soul. He looked down and saw Chief's Son's Hand hanging from around his neck, on his chest, each great ivory claw curved, there, the fur silky against the bright scarlet flannel. Such happiness broke up in him then he had to turn the complete circle to see everything once more in the beautiful world that had once been given him. Then he was going to lie down, and realized that he had no robe or even blanket to spread on the sand. He would arrive naked in the Green Grass World. Well, they would have an immediate opportunity to feel good by showing him their kindness. So he lay down then on the sand, his head to the north. It was very cold. He rolled onto his left side, pulled his knees up against the yellow claws. It was so quiet he could hear sand grains whisper to each other as they approached. For a long time he stared at the tiny world coming to him and for an instant he thought he would see, at last... but what he saw was the red shoulder of Sun at the rim of Earth, and he closed his eyes.

He felt the granular sand joined by snow running together, against and over him in delicate streams. It sifted over the crevices of his lips and eyes, between the folds of his face and hair and hands, legs; gradually rounded him over until there was a tiny mound on the sand hill almost imperceptible on the level horizon. Slowly, slowly, all changed continually into indistinguishable, as it seemed, and everlasting, unchanging, rock.

Indian graveyard, Fox Lake, with favourite possessions of the deceased left by relatives and friends.

# Excerpt from
## *THE VANISHING POINT*

by
W. O. Mitchell

Archie Nicotine stood before the Ladies and Escorts entrance of the Empress beer parlour. Forty-eight dollars — rings sixteen — carburetor from Hercules' Salvage — maybe eighteen — thirty — thirty-two — maybe fifteen over — ten anyway. Forty-eight. He could feel it almost warm against his left thigh — in his pocket there. Also he could use a beer. Way a man's tongue stuck to the roof of his mouth and his throat got stiff for the tickle of beer and the earth taste of beer.

A Hutterite passed him, turned into the Men's door; funny for them to be so religious, but you still saw a lot of black pail hats in any beer parlour all the same. His eyes idled over the passers-by — not one of them had to think twice about whether to go in and have a beer or not. Another man pushed past him and into the beer parlour. Denim smock — flat boots — farmer. Forty-eight — rings sixteen — carburetor eighteen. Twenty — fifteen dollars of beer was one hell of a lot of beer. Beer never hurt him — never hurt anybody. Let everyone suck it down and not a drop for him!

Red luck right from the start. There was the difference — how you were born was the whole situation. You either got born a horse or a foolhen or a link. Or red or white. His luck he got dropped red in the corner of a reservation bullfield, laced into moss in a *yo-kay-bo*, weaned on an elk bone. Tag around the tent or cabin — beans and bannock and tea when it was there — roll in or out when you felt like it — colt roping or grabbing hold of girls from thirteen on and "Onward Christian Soldiers" washed in the blood and all the white religions said no beer at all. With their flower-pot hats and their long noses and their twang, Latter Day Saints said it loudest. Mormon missionaries could ride and they could rope all right, but they got the coal oil onto their fire over beer — or even coffee — tea — Coke. So that washed up the L.D.S. How sweet the name of Jesus and the taste of beer — beer — beer — and the salt taste of beer cooling down your hot throat!

Sinclair was so smart; on his face you could tell he figured all the pole money would end up in the waiter's apron, then drunk and disorderly, and into the bucket before dark.

A Black and White taxi had stopped. A woman got out. High heels behind. And Sinclair said no laying hands on Esau too, so maybe he ought to just visit Heally Richards at that tent. Not with beer on his breath though. Tent. Church tent. Maybe it was some kind of a red religion from across the line with those little mushrooms you ate and they gave you a vision. Not very damn likely.

He caught a smell sweet as wolf willow, from the woman who pushed past him and into the Ladies and Escorts door of the Empress, her perfume winning over beer bloom through the opened door. Buh-beer — buh-beer — buh-beer — it beat in him like a Chicken Dance drum. The taxi was still at the curb, its driver, head down, making a notation on the seat beside himself. Sinclair was so smart pushing people around, so first thing was to go see Heally Richards to lay hands on old Esau — then Hercules Salvage for rings and the carburetor for the truck — then the Flying Saucer and Sinclair with surprise all over his face because he hadn't figured it out right at all.

He stepped across the street to the taxi. The driver looked out and up to him.

"You busy?"

"Get in." The driver leaned across and pushed open the front door.

Archie opened the back door and got in. The driver pulled shut the front door. He straightened up, tucked his note pad under the sun visor. He stared into the rear-view mirror. "Where to, Chief?"

The mirror framed the driver's eyes, his bridgeless nose — two punches of cheek bone; on the left one there was a faint linger of bruise. "I said where to, Chief?"

"The big tent."

"In the sky, that is."

"No. Other side the Stampede Grounds — just off Johnston Trail."

"Oh — that big tent." He thrust the car into gear and pulled away from the curb.

Sinclair could get one hell of a surprise. Come to think of it, he was a little surprised himself. "Turn south," he advised the driver as the car stopped at the Johnston Trail red light.

"I know, Chief. I know the way."

Maybe he ought to tell him how at fifteen he'd been top rider in the bareback and the calf roping — in the money for steer decorating — second highest — would have been all-round Little Britches Rodeo champion if it hadn't been for the saddle event.

"You Blood?"

"No."

"Sarcee?"

"No."

"Blackfoot."

"No."

Mary Rose Wagnan, smoking a moose hide, Fort Chipewyan. She is one of only a handful of women in the community who still hand tan in the traditional manner.

Old skiff, north shore of Lake Athabasca. The boat belonged to a native family and would have been their major means of transportation in a region where fishing, hunting, and trapping were a way of life.

Members of the Delta Native Fisherman's Association in Fort Chipewyan. Their locally owned and controlled fish plant ships pickerel to Winnipeg, from where it is distributed to markets as far away as Chicago.

Carl Granath cleans whitefish from his nets on Lake Athabasca.

"Sure as hell ain't Hooterite."

"You're correct," Archie said.

They had turned off Johnston Trail. The car did a double hiccup over the railroad tracks.

The tent was a lot bigger than it had looked from up above when he and Sinclair had driven into the city. Its khaki canvas scalloped above the slack guy ropes, swagging deep from the high poke of four poles. On the street side where the taxi had stopped, a framed banner said: GOD IS NOT DEAD!, the message centred in a curlicued margin of circus doodle decoration. It was as though the original portraits of freaks and wild animals had been painted out of the centre and the reassuring announcement substituted.

The meter read a dollar fifteen. Archie handed over a dollar and a quarter, waited till the driver leaned again to the opened window. "Thanks." The taxi driver dropped a dime into the hand Archie held out. "Chief."

"I'm not."

"Friendly form of address."

"It isn't."

"All right. Honest mistake then. Under the impression only chiefs could afford to ride taxis."

"I'm a duly elected band councillor."

"So you're travelling on an expense account. Red is beautiful."

"No, it isn't." Archie looked up to the baroque banner. "Guys like you it's the shits — and that is the whole situation."

He turned towards the revival tent so that he didn't hear what it was that the taxi driver growled, but a moment later he felt the angry pelt of gravel against the back of his leg.

Two men had just emerged from the tent opening. One was little; one, large. The Reverend Heally Richards was large, and he was also pure. His shoes, socks, pants, suit coat, vest, shirt, tie, made a white total in the spring sunlight. He could have been carved from lard except for his face; the white hair and white eyebrows, even the white eyelashes, jumped out from the darkly tanned face. The slight jowling of his cheeks, a fullness at the mouth, suggested beaver to Archie. The other man's totem had to be old mosquito. The Reverend Heally Richards was frowning, the old man talking, as they reached Archie.

"...isn't I'm complaining, Reverend Richards. That isn't it at all. When I came to the front last night for you to touch me ..."

"I recall I did, Brother Hillaker."

"I know you did, but I still had to get up seven times last night."

Richards' voice sounded just like it did on the radio. They had stopped, seemed quite unaware of Archie. And now the evangelist's big white back was to him; that was what made him think of the backward people. Anyone could heal people from being sick, a backward person might do it. Heally Richards should have walked backwards out of that tent.

"Isn't automatic, you know," Richards was saying.

"I know it isn't, Reverend."

"Nobody commands the Lord. You've got to understand that right now. You can't push Him around."

"No — no — I wouldn't — I don't want — but I figured if tonight you could touch me again..."

"Of course I will, Brother Hillaker — but first you have just got to understand this one thing — it is not for you to demand blessin' — or — is it for me — to guarantee — what the Lord does with His blessin'. After all..."

They had reached the street corner, turned, Heally walking quite quickly now. "You specialize in city people," Archie said.

"No — they come to me — people — from the city and from the country. They come to me."

Archie increased his pace. "Maybe I could catch a lift with you."

"If your destination is downtown — anywhere near the Devonian Tower."

"Not far," Archie said, and then he saw the Reverend Heally Richards' car.

"You're welcome, Brother — ah —"

"Nicotine," Archie said absently.

"Brother Nicotine." Heally Richards opened the car door. "Praise the Lord. Praise Him."

Cadillac! White! "Hallelujah!" Archie said fervently.

Roy Salopree, untitled, 1986, pen and ink.

# AUTUMN LIGHT

Maxwell Bates, *Road in the Foothills*, n.d., watercolour.

The Bow River at Exshaw.

*Opposite:*
Trembling aspen, Jasper.

Cypress Hills, looking towards Seven Persons. The Cree called this unique ecology *mi-n-ti-kak*, "beautiful upland." Early traders named it Montagne de Cyprès for its abundance of evergreens.

Fall road, Millarville.

Evening, Priddis.

West of Peace River.

Late summer, Jefferson, looking across the Montana border to Chief Mountain.

In the valley of the Bow, near Banff.

Cattle grazing, Old Man River valley, south of Iron Springs.

*Opposite:*
Near Grassy Lake.

The ghosts of November. A country road near the site of the St. Ann Ranch, established by a group of French cavalry officers in the vicinity of Trochu. Doomed romantics, they returned to fight in the Great War of 1914-18, from which few came back.

An early frost, Fort Saskatchewan.

Remembrance Day, Edmonton.

# FAR HORIZON

A. C. Leighton, *Prairie Town, Airdrie*, 1952, oil.

Elkwater, Cypress Hills.

# THE SKATING PARTY

by

Merna Summers

Our house looked down on the lake. From the east windows you could see it: a long sickle of blue, its banks hung with willow. Beyond was a wooded ridge which, like all such ridges in our part of the country, ran from northeast to southwest.

In another part of the world, both lake and ridge would have had names. Here, only people had names. I was Maida; my father was Will, my mother was Winnie. Take us all together and we were the Singletons. The Will Singletons, that is, as opposed to the Dan Singletons, who were my grandparents and dead, or Nathan Singleton, who was my uncle and lived in the city.

In the books I read, lakes and hills had names, and so did ponds and houses. Their names made them more real to me, of greater importance, than the hills and lakes and sloughs that I saw every day. I was eleven years old before I learned that the hill on which our house was built had once had a name. It was called Stone Man Hill. My parents had never thought to tell me that.

It was my uncle, Nathan Singleton, who told me. Uncle Nathan was a bachelor. He had been a teacher before he came to Willow Bunch, but he had wanted to be a farmer. He had farmed for a few years when he was a young man, on a quarter that was now part of our farm. His quarter was just south of what had been my grandfather's home place, and was now ours. But then he had moved to the city and become a teacher again.

In some ways it seemed as if he had never really left Willow Bunch. He spent all his holidays at our place, taking walks with me, talking to my mother, helping my father with such chores as he hadn't lost the knack of performing. Our home was his home. I found it hard to imagine him as I knew he must be in his classroom: wearing a suit, chalk dust on his sleeve, putting seat work on the blackboard. He didn't even talk like a teacher.

Uncle Nathan was older than my father, quite a lot older, but he didn't seem so to me. In some ways he seemed younger, for he told me things and my father did not. Not that my father was either silent or unloving. He talked as much as anybody, and he was fond of some people — me included — and showed it. What he did not give away was information.

Some children are sensitive: an eye and an ear and a taking-in of subtleties. I wasn't like that. I wanted to be told. I wanted to know how things really were and how people really acted. Sometimes it seemed to me that collecting the facts was uphill

work. I persisted because it was important for me to have them. I wanted to know who to praise and who to blame. Until I was in my mid-teens, that didn't seem to me to be too much to ask.

Perhaps my father had a reluctance to look at things too closely himself. He wanted to like people, and he may have found it easier to do if he kept them a little out of focus. Besides that, he believed that life was something that children should be protected from knowing about for as long as possible.

I got most of my information from my mother. She believed that knowledge *was* protection: that children had a right to know and parents had an obligation to teach. She didn't know all there was to know, but what she did know she intended to pass on to me.

I knew this because I heard her say so one night after I had gone to bed. Uncle Nathan, who was at the farm for the weekend, saw things my mother's way. "What you don't know *can* hurt you," he said. "Especially what you don't know about yourself."

So my mother and my uncle talked to me, both as sort of inoculation against life and because, I now believe, both of them liked to talk anyway. I was always willing to listen. My father listened too. He might feel that my mother told me too much, but his conviction wasn't strong enough to stop her.

It was Uncle Nathan, talking for pleasure, not policy, who gave me the pleasure of knowing that I lived in a place with a name. Stone Man Hill was so named, he said, because long ago there had existed on the slopes below our house the shape of a man, outlined in fieldstones.

"He was big," Uncle Nathan said. "Maybe fifteen yards, head to foot."

It was a summer afternoon. I was eleven. My father, in from the fields for coffee, was sitting at the kitchen table. His eyelashes were sooty with field dust. My mother was perched on a kitchen stool by the cupboard, picking over berries.

"He must have been quite a sight," my father said.

I walked to the east window of the kitchen and looked out. Trying to imagine our hillside field of brome as unbroken prairie sod, trying to picture what a stone man would look like stretched out among the buffalo beans and gopher holes, his face to the sky.

"You get me a writing pad and I'll show you what he looked like," Uncle Nathan said.

I got the pad and Uncle Nathan sat down at the table opposite my father. I sat beside him, watching as he began to trace a series of dots. His hand worked quickly, as if the dots were already visible, but only to his eyes. The outline of a man took shape.

"Who made the stone man?" I asked.

"Indians," Uncle Nathan said. He held the picture up, as if considering additions. "But I don't know when and I don't know why."

"He could have been there a hundred years," my father said. "Maybe more. There was no way of telling."

"I used to wonder why the Indians chose this hill," Uncle Nathan said. "I still do."

He got up and walked to the window, looking out at the hill and the lake and the ridge. "It may be that it was some sort of holy place to them," he said.

My mother left the cupboard and came across to the table. She picked up Uncle Nathan's drawing. Looking at it, the corners of her mouth twitched upwards.

"You're sure you haven't forgotten anything?" she asked. "Your mother used to say the stone man was *very* complete."

Uncle Nathan returned her smile. "The pencil's right here, Winnie," he said. "You're welcome to it."

My father spoke quickly, "It was too bad the folks didn't have a camera," he said. "It would have been nice to have a picture of the stone man."

My mother went back to her berries.

"I've always been sorry I was too young to remember him," my father said. "Before he turned into a rock pile, that is."

I hadn't yet got around to wondering about the stone man's disappearance. Now I did. He should still have been on his hillside for me to look at. My father had been a baby when his people came to Willow Bunch, and he couldn't remember the stone man. My uncle had been a young man and could. But the difference in their ages and experience hadn't kept them from sharing a feeling of excitement at the thought of a stone man on our hillside. Why had my grandfather been insensible to this appeal? Hadn't he liked the stone man?

"Liking wouldn't enter into it," my father said. "Your grandfather had a family to feed. He knew where his duty lay."

"There was thirty acres broke when Pa bought this place," Uncle Nathan said. "He thought he needed more. And this hill was the only land he could break without brushing it first."

Somebody else had owned our place before my grandfather,

hadn't they? I asked. He hadn't turned the stone man into a rock pile.

"He was a bachelor," my father said.

"The way your grandfather saw it," Uncle Nathan said, "it was a case of wheat or stones. And he chose wheat."

"Which would you have chosen?" I asked Uncle Nathan. "Which did you want?"

"I wanted both," Uncle Nathan said.

"The choice wasn't yours to make." My mother spoke as if she were defending him.

"That's what I thought then," Uncle Nathan said. "I thought when Pa told me to get those rocks picked, that that was what I had to do. I think now I should have spoken up. I know for years I felt guilty whenever I remembered that I had done just what was expected of me."

He looked up, a half-smile on his face. "I know it sounds crazy," he said, "but I felt as if the stone man had more claim on me than my own father did."

"We all of us think some crazy things sometimes," my father said.

Near Clairmont.

*Opposite:*
Sledding on the outskirts of Beaumont. The town was named because of the superb view of the surrounding countryside from the hill on which the town is built.

Rolly View slough hockey.

Albert Roesch, 82, fishing in January on the last open water on the Battle River.

From my point of view, Uncle Nathan had only one peculiarity. He had never married. And though I sometimes asked him why, I never found any satisfaction in his answers.

"Maybe it wasn't every girl who took my eye," he told me once. "I'd pity the girl who had to count on me to take care of her," he said another time.

Then my parents told me about the skating party. It had been a dark night in November, and my mother, five years old, had come to our lake with her parents, and spent the night pushing a kitchen chair in front of her across the ice, trying to learn to skate. The party was being held in honour of Uncle Nathan and a girl called Eunice Lathem. They were to be married soon, and their friends planned, after the skating, to go up to the house to present a gift to them. The gift and the fact that the party was in her honour were to be a surprise to Eunice. Nathan, for some reason, had been told about it.

There had been cold that year but no snow, so you could skate all over the lake. My mother remembered them skimming by, the golden lads and girls who made up the world when she was small, and Nathan and Eunice the most romantic of all. Nathan was handsome and Eunice was beautiful and they were very much in love, she said.

She remembered the skaters by moonlight, slim black shapes mysterious against the silver fields. There were a lot of clouds in the sky that night and when the moon went behind one of them, friends, neighbours and parents' friends became alike: all equally unknown, unidentifiable.

My grandfather and Uncle Nathan had built a big wood fire at the near end of the lake. My mother said that it was a grand experience to skate off into the darkness and the perils and dangers of the night, and then turn and come back towards the light, following the fire's reflection on the ice.

Late on, when some people were already making their way up the hill to the house, Eunice Lathem went skating off into the darkness with her sister. They didn't skate up the middle of the lake as most of the skaters had been doing. Instead they went off toward the east bank. There is a place there where a spring rises and the water is deep, but they didn't know that. The ice was thinner there. They broke through.

Near the fire, people heard their cries for help. A group of the men skated out to rescue them. When the men got close to the place where the girls were in the water, the ice began to crack under their feet.

All the men lay down then and formed a chain, each holding the ankles of the man in front of him, Uncle Nathan was at the front. He inched forward, feeling the ice tremble beneath his body, until he came to the point where he could reach either of two pairs of hands clinging to the fractured edge.

It was dark. He couldn't see the girls' faces. All he could do was grasp the nearest pair of wrists and pull. The men behind him pulled on his feet. Together they dragged one girl back to safety. But as they were doing it, the ice broke away beneath them and the second girl went under. The moon came out and they saw it was Eunice Lathem's sister they had saved. They went back to the hole, but Eunice had vanished. There wasn't any way they could even get her body.

"It was an awful thing to have happen on our place," my father said.

"Your Uncle Nathan risked his life," my mother said. Her voice was earnest, for she too believed in identifying heroes and villains.

"There was no way on earth he could save both girls," she said. "The ice was already breaking, and the extra weight of the first one was bound to be too much for it."

Why hadn't he saved Eunice first?

"I told you," my mother said. "He couldn't see their faces."

It troubled me that he hadn't had some way of knowing. I would have expected love to be able to call out to love. If it couldn't do that, what was it good for? And why had the moon been behind a cloud anyway?

"Your grandmother used to say that the Lord moves in a mysterious way," my father said.

"What does that mean?" I asked.

"It means that nobody knows," my mother said.

I'd seen Eunice Lathem's name on a grave in the yard of St. Chad's, where we attended services every second Sunday. If I'd thought of her at all, it was as a person who had always been dead. Now she seemed real to me, almost like a relative. She was a girl who had loved and been loved. I began to make up stories about her. But I no longer skated on the lake alone.

Eunice Lathem's sister, whose name was Delia Sykes, moved away from Willow Bunch right after the accident. She didn't wait until her husband sold out; she went straight to Edmonton and waited for him there. Even when they buried Eunice in the spring, she didn't come back.

Storm gathering above Timber Ridge in the Foothills, west of Nanton.

George Robertson attends to a Saturday morning customer in his barber shop and pool room, Delburne.

Years later, someone from Willow Bunch had seen her in Edmonton. She didn't mention Eunice or the accident or even Willow Bunch.

"It must have been a short conversation," my mother said practically.

Is it surprising that I continued to wonder why Uncle Nathan didn't marry? Some people remember their childhoods as a time when they thought of anybody over the age of twenty-five as being so decrepit as to be beyond all thought of romance or adventure. I remember feeling that way about *women*, but I never thought of men that way, whatever their ages. It seemed to me that Uncle Nathan could still pick out a girl and marry her if he set his mind to it.

"No," he said when I asked him. "Not 'still' and not 'pick out a girl.' A person doesn't have that much say in the matter. You can't love where you choose."

And then, making a joke of it, "See that you remember that when your time comes," he said.

One day my mother showed me a picture of Eunice Lathem and her sister. Two girls and a pony stood looking at the camera. Both girls were pretty. The one who wasn't Eunice was laughing; she looked like a girl who loved to laugh. Eunice was pretty too, but there was a stillness about her, almost a sternness. If she hadn't been Eunice Lathem, I would have said she was sulking.

I felt cheated. Was the laughing one also prettier?

"She may have been," my mother said. "I remember Eunice Lathem as being beautiful. But since Delia Sykes was married, I don't suppose I gave her looks a thought one way or the other."

As I grew older I spent less time wondering about the girl who'd been Eunice Lathem. I'd never wondered about her sister, and perhaps never would have if I hadn't happened to be with Uncle Nathan the day he heard that Delia Sykes had died.

It was the spring I was fifteen. My parents were away for the weekend, attending a silver wedding in Rochfort Bridge. Uncle Nathan and I were alone on the farm and so, if he wanted to talk about Delia Sykes, he hadn't much choice about who to talk to.

It was a morning for bad news. The frost was coming out of the ground, setting the very ditches and wheel-ruts to weeping. Out in the barn, a ewe was mourning her lost lamb. We had put her in a pen by herself and we were saving the dead lamb, so we could use its skin to dress another lamb in case one of the ewes died in lambing or had no milk.

Uncle Nathan and I left the barn and walked out to the road to pick up the mail. The news of Delia's death was in the local paper. "Old-timers will be saddened to learn of the death in Duncan, B.C. of Mrs. Delia Sykes, a former resident of this district," the paper said.

Uncle Nathan shook his head slowly, as if he found the news hard to believe. "So Delia's gone," he said. "She was a grand girl, Delia Sykes. No matter what anybody said, she was a grand girl."

There was a picture of Mrs. Sykes with the death notice. I saw a middle-aged woman who had gone from the hair-dresser's to the photographer's. Her cheeks were as firm and round as two peach halves, and she had snappy eyes. She was wearing a white dress. She looked as if she might have belonged to the Eastern Star or the Rebekahs.

Uncle Nathan looked at the picture too. "Delia always was a beauty," he said.

He sat in silence for a while, and then, bit by bit, he began to tell me the story of how he had met Delia Sykes and before her, her husband.

"Only I didn't realize that he was her husband," Uncle Nathan said. "I thought when I met her that she was single; that was the joke of it."

It was late July and late afternoon. Uncle Nathan was teaching school, to make enough money to live on until his farm got going. But he was hoping to get out of it.

"The land was new then and we thought there was no limit to how rich we were all going to be some day. Besides that," he added, "what I wanted to do was farm. School-teaching seemed to me to be no proper job for a man."

There were two things Uncle Nathan wanted. One was to stop teaching. The other was to find a wife.

There were more men than girls around then, he told me, so the man who wanted a good selection had to be prepared to cover a lot of territory.

"Harold Knight and I took in dances and ball games as far away as Hasty Hills," he said.

*Opposite:*
Fields drifted by a wind that seldom stops, north of Lundbreck.

Below Grouard Mission, Buffalo Bay, Lesser Slave Lake.

They'd already seen a fair sampling, but there were still girls they hadn't seen.

"I had a pretty fair idea of what I was looking for," Uncle Nathan said. "I imagine it was the same sort of thing every young fellow thinks he's looking for, but I thought I had standards. I wasn't willing to settle for just anyone."

It was with the idea of looking over another couple of girls that he went to see Harold Knight that late July afternoon. A family with two daughters was rumoured to have moved in somewhere near Morningside School. He'd come to suggest to Harold that they take in the church service at the school the next Sunday.

The Knights, Uncle Nathan said, had hay and seed wheat to sell to people with the money to buy it. When Uncle Nathan walked into their yard that day, he saw that Mr. Knight was talking to a buyer. It was a man he'd never seen before, but he guessed by the cut of the man's rig that he must be well fixed.

"Nathan," Mr. Knight said, "meet Dobson Sykes."

Mr. Sykes was a straight-standing man with greying hair. He put out his hand and Uncle Nathan shook it.

"His driving horses," Uncle Nathan said, "were as showy a team as I'd ever seen — big bays with coats the colour of red willow."

"You'd go a long way before you'd find a better-matched team than that," Mr. Knight said.

"Oh, they match well enough." Dobson Sykes spoke as if that was a matter of little importance to him, as if no effort was made in the acquiring of such a team. "I'd trade them in a minute if something better came along," he said carelessly. "I have a job to keep Spark, here, up to his collar."

"I had a fair amount of respect then for men who'd done well in life," Uncle Nathan told me. "This man was about my father's age, old enough to have made it on his own. When a man like that came my way, I studied him. I thought if I was going to be a farmer instead of a teacher, I'd have to start figuring out how people went about getting things in life.

"I wasn't really surprised when Mr. Knight said that Sykes had a crew of men — men he was paying — putting up a set of buildings for him on a place he'd bought near Bannock Hill. He looked like a man with that kind of money."

"We're not building anything fancy," Dobson Sykes said. "If I'd wanted to stay farming on a big scale, I wouldn't have moved from Manitoba."

After a while Uncle Nathan left the two older men talking and walked out toward the meadow, where Harold was fetching a load of hay for Mr. Sykes.

It was on the trail between buildings and meadow that he met Delia Sykes.

He didn't see her at first because she wasn't sitting up front with Harold. She must have been lying back in the hay, Uncle Nathan said, just watching the clouds drift by overhead. She sat up.

Uncle Nathan saw at once that she was not very old; he had girls almost as old as she was in his classroom. But there was nothing of the schoolgirl about Delia. She was young but womanly. Everything about her curved, from the line of her cheek to the way she carried her arms.

Uncle Nathan saw all this in the instant that she appeared looking down over the edge of the load. He saw too that she had a kind of class he'd never seen around Willow Bunch. She

looked like a girl perfectly suited to riding around the country behind a team of perfectly matched bays.

She reached behind her into the hay and came up with a crown of french-braided dandelions. She set it on top of her hair and smiled.

He knew right then, Uncle Nathan said, that his voice wouldn't be among those swelling the hymns at Morningside School next Sunday. And he felt as if he understood for the first time how men must feel when they are called to the ministry. Choosing and decision and standards have nothing to do with it. You're called or you're not called, and when you're called you know it.

The girl smiled and opened her arms as if to take in the clouds in the sky and the bees buzzing in the air and the red-topped grasses stirring in the wind. Then she spoke.

"You've got no worries on a load of hay," she said.

Those were the first words Uncle Nathan heard Delia Sykes say. "You've got no worries on a load of hay."

There was a patch of milkweed blooming near the path where Uncle Nathan was standing. In late July, small pink blossoms appear and the milk, rich and white, is ready to run as soon as you break the stalk. Uncle Nathan picked a branch, climbed the load of hay, and presented it to the girl.

"It's not roses," he said, "but the sap is supposed to cure warts."

She laughed. "My name is Delia Sykes," she said.

"I thought she was Dobson's daughter," Uncle Nathan said, "and it crossed my mind to wonder if he'd have traded her off if she hadn't moved along smart in her harness.

"There didn't seem to be much fear of that. You could see right away she had spirit. If she had too much, it was nothing that marriage to a good man wouldn't cure, I thought."

Uncle Nathan gave a rueful smile. "Of course when we got back to the yard I found out that she wasn't Dobson's daughter but his wife. Later I wondered why she hadn't introduced herself as *Mrs.* Sykes. And she'd called me *Nathan* too, and girls didn't do that then.

"The truth is," Uncle Nathan said, "I had kind of fallen for her."

Did she feel the same way about him?

If she did, Uncle Nathan wasn't willing to say so. "Delia was only nineteen," he said. "I don't think she knew what she wanted."

He was silent for a while. Then he went on with his story. "Once I knew she was married," he said, "I knew right away what I had to do. I remember I gave myself a good talking to. I said, 'If you can fall in love in twenty minutes, you can fall out of love just as fast.'"

"And could you?"

"Some people could, I guess," Uncle Nathan said. "It seemed to take me a bit longer."

The story stopped then because we had to go out to the barn to check the sheep. While we'd been in the house, another ewe had dropped her lamb. We heard it bleat as we came in the barn, and the ewe whose lamb had died heard it too. It was at the far end of the barn, out of sight, but at the sound of it, milk began to run from her udder. She couldn't help herself.

We checked the rest of the sheep and then we went back into the house. I made us a pot of tea.

"I was afraid to go and see Dobson and Delia after they got moved in," Uncle Nathan said. "I think I was afraid somebody would read my mind."

He went, he said, because Delia soon made her house a gathering place for all the young people of the district, and he didn't see how he could be the only one to stay away. Delia didn't make things any easier for him.

"She used to keep saying she'd only been married three months . . . as if that made it any less final. And when she spoke of anything they had — whether it was a buggy or a kitchen safe or the pet dog — she would say 'my buggy' or 'my kitchen safe' or 'my dog'. 'We' and 'us' were words she didn't use at all."

I poured our tea then, trying to imagine the house that Delia Sykes had lived in.

"It was something of a showplace for its time," Uncle Nathan told me. Everything in it was the best of its kind, he said, from the Home Comfort stove in the kitchen to the pump organ in the parlour. What puzzled Uncle Nathan was Delia's attitude to her things. She'd picked them out herself in Winnipeg and ordered them sent, but when they got here, she seemed to feel they weren't important.

"The more things you've got, the more things you've got to take care of," she said. She didn't even unpack most of her trunks.

Dobson was worried. He thought that moving away from her family had unsettled her. "Delia wasn't like this in Manitoba," he said.

"I kept wondering," Uncle Nathan said, "where we would go from here. It never occurred to me that there could be another girl for me. And then Eunice came along."

It was on an October afternoon, Uncle Nathan said, that he met Eunice Lathem.

The sun was low in the southwest when he drove into the Sykes yard, and Dobson, as usual, was out around the buildings showing the younger men his grinding mill, his blacksmith shop, his threshing machine.

Uncle Nathan remembered that the trees were leafless except for the plumes of new growth at the top. He tied up his horse and, as he headed for the house, saw that the afternoon sun was turning the west-facing walls all gold and blue. It looked like a day for endings, not beginnings. But he went into the house, and there stood Eunice Lathem.

Eunice was a year or two older than Delia but she looked just like her. Uncle Nathan noticed that she was quieter.

Supper was already on the table when Uncle Nathan got there. The news of Eunice's arrival had attracted such a company of bachelors that there weren't enough plates or chairs for everybody to eat at once.

"I don't know about anybody else, but I'm starving," Delia announced, taking her place at the head of the table. Eunice, though she was the guest of honour, insisted on waiting until the second sitting.

As the first eaters prepared to deal with their pie, Eunice began to ladle water out of a stoneware crock into a dishpan. Uncle Nathan went to help her. He said something funny and she laughed.

Delia's voice startled them both. "I invited Eunice out here to find a husband," she said with a high-pitched laugh. "I said to myself, 'With all the bachelors we've got around, if she can't find a husband here, there's no hope for her.'"

Delia spoke as if she were making a joke, and there was a nervous round of laughter. Blood rose in Eunice's face.

"If I'd known that was why you were asking me," Eunice said, "I would never have come."

And indeed, Uncle Nathan said, Eunice wasn't the sort of girl to need anyone's help in finding a husband. She was, if anything, prettier than Delia. Not as showy, perhaps, perhaps not as rounded. But if you went over them point by point comparing noses, chins, teeth and all the rest of it, Eunice might well have come out on top.

Later, when the others had gone, Delia apologized. "I

shouldn't have said that," she said. "It sounded awful." She didn't even claim to have been making a joke.

"I want you two to be friends," she said.

In the weeks that followed, Uncle Nathan saw that Delia was pushing her sister his way. He didn't know why, but he didn't find the idea unpleasant.

"I suppose I liked Eunice at first because she looked so much like Delia," he said, "but as I got to know her better it seemed to me that she might be easier to get along with in the long run. I wouldn't be the first man to marry the sister of the girl who first took his fancy, nor the last one either.

"It seemed to me that a man could love one girl as easily as another if he put his mind to it. I reasoned it out. How much did the person matter anyway? That was what I asked myself. It seemed to me that when all was said and done, it would be the life that two people made together that would count, not who the people were.

"I remembered thinking that getting married would be like learning to dance. Some people are born knowing how; they have a natural beat. Other people have to make an effort to learn. But all of them, finally, are moving along to the music one way or the other.

"Anyway," Uncle Nathan said, "I spoke to Eunice, and she agreed, and we decided to be married at Christmas.

"It was September, I think, when we got engaged," Uncle Nathan said. "I remember thinking about telling Dobson and Delia. I could imagine the four of us — Dobson and Delia, Eunice and me — living side by side, spending our Sundays together, raising children who would be cousins and might even look like each other.

"I came over early on the Sunday and we told them. Delia didn't have very much to say then. But in the afternoon when quite a crowd had gathered and Eunice and I were waiting for the rest of them to get there before we made our announcement, a strange thing happened.

"The day before, Dobson had brought home a new saddle pony and Delia had wanted to ride it. Dobson didn't know how well broke it was, or if it could be trusted, and he refused. I guess that refusal rankled. Delia didn't like to be told she couldn't do a thing or have a thing she had set her heart on.

"Anyway, on Sunday afternoon Eunice was sitting at the pump organ playing for us, and she looked beautiful. We were all sitting around looking at her.

"And then somebody happened to glance out of the win-

Canyon Creek, on the south shore of Lesser Slave Lake.

dow," Uncle Nathan said. "And there was Delia on the pony, and the pair of them putting on a regular rodeo.

"She didn't break her neck, which was a wonder. By the time she finally got off the pony, we were all out in the yard, and somebody had the idea of taking a picture of Delia and Eunice and the pony."

After that, Uncle Nathan said, Delia seemed to want to get the wedding over with as soon as possible. She hemmed sheets and ordered linen and initialled pillow-cases. When November finally came and the neighbours decided on a skating party for Eunice and Uncle Nathan, it was Delia who sewed white rabbit fur around the sleeves and bottom of Eunice's coat, so that it would look like a skating dress.

The night of the party was dark. There was a moon, but the sky was cloudy. They walked down the hill together, all those young people, laughing and talking.

"One minute you could see their faces and the next they would all disappear," Uncle Nathan said. "I touched a match to a bonfire we had laid in the afternoon, and we all sat down to screw on our skates.

"I skated first with Eunice. She wanted to stay near the fire so we could see where we were going. I skated with several other girls, putting off, for some reason, the time when I would skate with Delia. But then she came gliding up to me and held out her hands, and I took them and we headed out together into the darkness.

"As soon as we turned our backs on the fire it was as if something came over us. We wanted to skate out farther and farther. It seemed to me that we could keep on like this all our lives, just skating outward farther and farther, and the lake would keep getting longer and longer so that we would never come to the end of it."

Uncle Nathan sighed. "I didn't know then that in three days Delia would have left Willow Bunch for good, and in six months I would have followed her," he said.

Why had he given up farming?

"Farming's no life for a man alone," he said. "And I couldn't imagine ever wanting to marry again."

He resumed his story. "Once the moon came out and I could see Delia's face, determined in the moonlight.

" 'Do you want to turn back?' I asked her.

" ' I'm game as long as you are,' she said.

"Another time, 'I don't ever want to turn back,' she said.

"I gave in before Delia did," Uncle Nathan said. " ' If we don't turn around pretty soon,' I told her, 'we're going to be skating straight up Pa's stubble fields.'

"We turned around then, and there was the light from the fire and our feet already set on its path. And I found I wanted to be back there with all the people around me. Eunice deserved better, and I knew it."

As they came toward the fire, Eunice skated out to meet them. "I might as well have been someplace else for all the attention she paid me," Uncle Nathan said. Her words were all for Delia.

"If this is what you got me out here for," Eunice said, "you can just forget about it. I'm not going to be your window blind."

"I don't know what you're talking about," Delia said.

She looked unhappy. "She knew as well as I did," Uncle Nathan said, "that whatever we were doing out there, it was more than just skating."

"We were only skating," Delia said. And then her temper rose. "You always were jealous of me," she said.

"Who would you say was jealous now?" Eunice asked.

"We were far enough away from the fire for the girls not to be heard," Uncle Nathan said. "At least I hoped we were.

"What was worrying me was the thought of Eunice having to meet all the people up at the house, and finding out she was the guest of honour, and having to try to rise to the occasion.

"That was why I suggested that the two of them go for a skate. I thought it would give them a chance to cool down. Besides," he added, "I couldn't think of anything else to do."

The girls let themselves be persuaded. They skated off together and Uncle Nathan watched them go. First he could see their two silhouettes, slim and graceful against the silver lake. Then all he could see was the white fur on Eunice's coat. And then they were swallowed up by the darkness.

"It was several minutes before we heard them calling for help," Uncle Nathan said.

Uncle Nathan and I sat silent for some time then: he remembering, I pondering. "If only you could have seen how beautiful she was," he said at last, and I didn't know whether it was Eunice he was speaking of, or Delia.

"I wonder if I would have felt any better about it if I'd got Eunice instead of Delia," he said. I realized that he'd been trying to make the judgement for thirty years.

"You didn't have any choice," I reminded him. "It was dark. You couldn't see their faces."

"No," Uncle Nathan said. "I couldn't see their faces." The sound of old winters was in his voice, a sound of infinite sadness.

"But I could see their hands on the edge of the ice," he said. "The one pair of arms had white fur around them.

"And I reached for the other pair."

James Agrell-Smith, *Horses, Wind and Dust*, 1961, wood engraving.

# THE MIND'S EYE

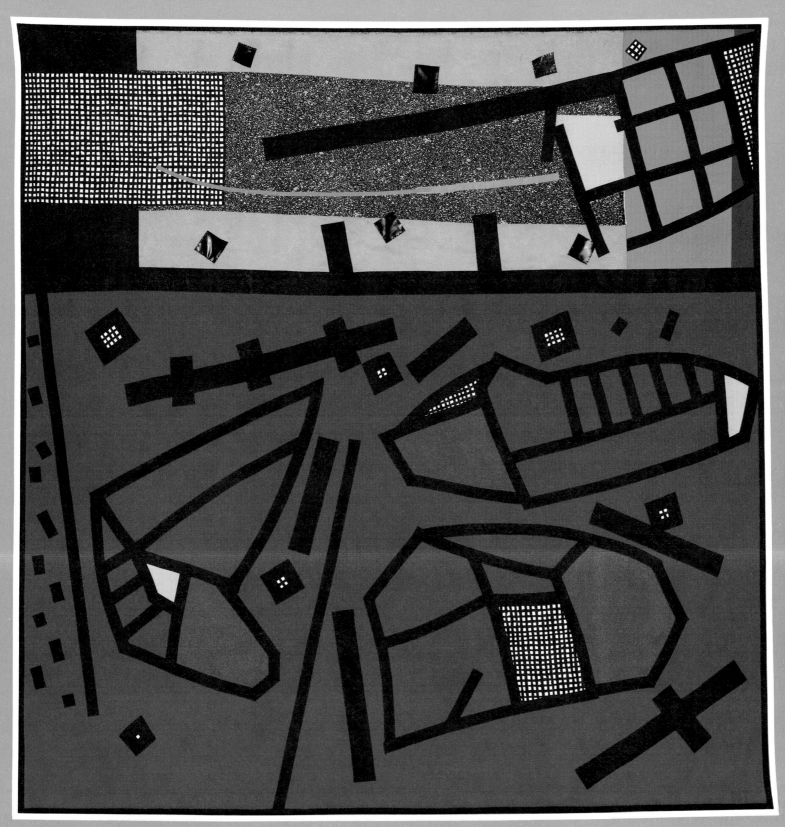

Wendy Toogood, *Float*, 1986, fabric.

# MASTER OF ARTS

by
Caterina Edwards

True art is slow to grow.
Like a belated friend,
It comes to let one know
Of what has had an end.

*Yvor Winters*

I was invited to read a few poems at my alma mater as a part of a celebration of successful creative writing graduates. I was thrilled, almost justified, simply because my success was relative: three books of poetry from small presses, readings in cafés and bookstores, reviews that were positive, never ecstatic. The night before the reading I slept badly and on the day, I spent hours deciding what to wear and whether my hair should be up or down. I had carefully worked out a sequence of poems and practised before my children, who giggled, and the babysitter, who was solemn with respect. But as soon as I was introduced, as soon as I took my place at the lectern, I knew I was all wrong. That audience: the students, sure they were the literary masters of the future, the academics, confident they were on the "cutting edge", the public, in search of contact with celebrity; that audience wanted pyrotechnical flash: language games, chants or, at least, a psychological strip tease, not sober-suited me and my sober-minded poems. That audience wanted to be anointed as the élite. And it waited, wanting. While I stood, struggling to speak, I tried my best smile. "I don't know if you're ready for this." The words slipped out. I could no longer see the rows of faces, but I could hear the shifting in the chairs, the first whispers. Each word of my introduction was isolated by parenthetical pauses. Finally I opened the book and fell into a particularly convoluted poem I hadn't intended to read.

The three poets who had read before me had given more practised performances. The first was a woman, a contemporary of mine. She used the seductive form: red silk, breathless voice, intimate smiles and hints of aberration. She fractured words, dividing them back into syllables. "Pen on paper/pen e trating/pen"—repeating and repeating, demystifying, deconstructing de de de, her body, her book. (She, not I, was a true warm-up act.)

The second reader with his eight books of poetry and national publisher was the unofficial star of the evening. He

had decided to sit in the back row and not on the stage with the rest of us. On being introduced, he strode forward, leaping up the steps. Once on the stage, he paced, trailing smoke and angst, stopping only for the ashtray and a long, troubled look at the audience. He flashed his sensitivity and his suffering. It was so tough this wrestling the cosmos for meaning, so *hard* to be so profound about the mind, consciousness, bipolarity, the subliminal, paradigms, and even quantum mechanics. And he was willing to give, to share, tossing each pellet of a word at the uncomprehending but titillated audience.

David, an old friend, was the third reader. I did not manage to follow even one of his poems. Halfway through the star's well-worn act (that eighties version of the poet as sexual prophet in the wilderness of Philistines), I had stopped listening. My unease with the first two readings, my nervousness as mine approached and David's proximity, his hand on the table, his shoulder, his smell (the aftershave I remembered so well), all drew me away. I kept the appropriate intrigued and attentive pose, but inside I was back twenty years, just starting university.

All my memories of that beginning are golden — ten carat at least. I can still see myself, so self aware, walking across campus, my books under my arm. How pleased I was with the old ivy covered buildings, the multitude of trees, with the flip of my dark green kilt (as seen in *Seventeen*), and with my serious expression as I settled at a table in Rutherford library. I had found my appropriate setting. The fears, the depressions, the tensions between what was expected of me and what I wanted to do were all behind me in the small prairie town I came from. I was prepared for a sparkling future.

The requisite man also turned up that first week. David sat across from me in Latin 200 and the first time he smiled at one of the professor's jokes, I quite forgot myself. When he stopped me on my way to the library and suggested coffee and cinnamon buns, it was the beginning of the end of serious settling at Rutherford.

Ensconced at a booth at Tuckshop, I asked him his major. His answer glittered: he was a graduate student in English. "But I'm going to write. None of that academic shit either, not for me. I'm a poet." He did smile a bit sheepishly. "Staring into the face of the abyss, plumbing the depths, real work." And then he asked me to the poetry reading, "a new experience for you."

My first date, not technically, of course, but my first date

Calgary Sculptor Katie von der Ohe was born in Peers, Alberta. She has won numerous awards for her work, which utilizes a variety of materials from plastic to steel.

Rudy Wiebe, novelist and winner of a Governor General's Award for *The Temptations of Big Bear*.

Marion Nicholl, *Prophet*, 1960, oil on canvas.

without my little sister giggling "couldn't you do better than that?", without hovering parents, without "his shoes needed shining," "he had two stains on his shirt," "No manners, he didn't shake hands. He just stood like a piece of dried codfish." "Weren't you going to study tonight?" Without "And your scholarship? If you start running around. . . " "We were about to call the police. What do you mean it's only twelve? Do you have any idea of the worry. . . "

My first date and my first week at university. I sat on my bed in my tiny room and traced the slightly curling edge of the old wallpaper, a trellis of faded yellow roses climbing the walls, up and down. When I turned my head and stared across at the bureau mirror, my reflection was framed by the delicate, still perky roses. I was defined, gift wrapped, my life the present.

A soft knock on my door and, before I could answer, Beppi was in the room. He was the seven-year-old son of two family friends, Cesare and Maria, in whose house I was boarding.

"There's a man downstairs that wants you."

"Oh, I'm not quite ready." I picked up my eyeshadow brush. "Can you tell him I'll be down in a few minutes?"

"Why are you putting that stuff on? You don't other times." He was sticking a finger in the powder then running the finger

along on the edge of the bureau. "Are you excited? You seem excited."

I swatted the air over his hand. "Don't. Come on. Go tell him. Please." Beppi was inspecting the other boxes, his face twisted into a showy, disgusted expression. I lifted him by the armpits and deposited him outside my door. "Please. I need just a couple of minutes."

When I finally came down the stairs, I found David sprawled out at the bottom. Three-year-old Mimma was on his back, trying both to ride him and use him as a shield. Beppi and Cesare were on the other side of the entrance, showering David and Mimma with plastic blocks. David was tossing the missiles back, growling.

I waited on the stairs, I tried a hello, but no one seemed to hear. Mimma was screeching, her father letting out a few dramatic roars. I nudged David with my foot and, when he didn't turn to me, shook his shoulder.

He looked then, smiled, but held up his hand, palm out, to hold me off. They kept on: yelling and throwing, approaching and retreating. It was Cesare who stopped first. "Enough. Come on, little monsters, time to clean up."

"I'm the guest." David had the most open, happy smile I had ever seen. "I don't have to."

Cesare stood up, his face flushed, and extended his hand to David. "I'll have to think twice about inviting you in next time."

David leaned over his bag, which had been stowed under the hall table, and pulled out a large, metal object crowned with a bright pink bow. "For you." He plopped it into my lap. "In honor of our first date."

The metal mass was a man on a horse.

"It's Don Quixote."

"I figured that. . . It's terrific. . . Really."

"I thought we could tilt at windmills together."

"Tilt? Sure. Yes. Of course."

The reading was scheduled for a large lounge in the old Students' Union Building. We arrived on time. The room was full, the reader nowhere to be seen. We had to go right up to the front row for a seat. As we made our way, David waved, called out and paused. "This is Susanna, Susanna meet. . . I found her in Latin class. Just sitting there." The men were bearded, turtle-necked, the women in black leotards, black skirts and with black lines around their eyes. Although it was the mid-sixties, the group (I was later to realize) was the remnant of the local beat generation. The women wove or batiked, took modern dance lessons, served Greek food in dark earthenware, and longed for "anywhere but here." The men smoked pipes, wrote poetry and complained incessantly about Edmonton and the Social Credit government. They had massive stereos and massive record collections. They all went to the Film Society and to the Yardbird Suite for jazz and avant-garde plays that did away with the traditional idea of characters.

Besides knowing each other, they all knew the woman who was to read. She wasn't introduced. She was suddenly there, a tiny figure in a flowing green robe. She waited impassively, eyes half closed, for silence, for attention. When the chatter and shushes faded, she flicked open her eyes, tilted her head back and ran her fingers haphazardly through her pixyish hair so that a few random clumps stuck up.

"I don't know." She paused, her eyes raking the audience. "I just don't know if you're ready for this." They were. As she launched into an intense version of "Daddy", as she seriously, dramatically, recounted the facts of Sylvia Plath's life, as she chanted "Lady Lazarus", as she read one of her own poems where she suggested that Sylvia had been killed by the establishment of male poets, the audience was with her. They sat in respectful silence at each pause, and they responded to the beginning of each poem with sighs and murmurs, the way a pop audience claps when it recognizes the opening bars of an old hit.

It was I who was not ready. I don't know how I would have reacted if I had read those poems before hearing them, but that day, listening, I was overcome with an embarrassment that was almost shame. For those words and the emotions they carried spoke to what was most dark and most private in me. Inside was suddenly outside — and exposed, magnified.

Over the next couple of years I gradually became familiar with and a part of David's group and the university. I also became familiar with Sylvia's poems, rereading them so often that I could recite stanzas at will. A novelist I respect, when speaking of how she became the writer she is, mentions a time when she would recite certain phrases such as "I dress in brown" and "Ah, Isabella is leaving" and feel immensely happy. I too would murmur certain phrases to myself over and over — "Daddy, daddy, you bastard I'm through" or "I eat men like air." And I would feel not so much happiness as pleasure. I had lost that first sense of violation. Now the words and the

A musical family. Thomas Rolston, violinist, and Isabel Moore, pianist, teachers at the Banff Centre, and their daughter, internationally acclaimed cellist, Shauna Rolston.

tone seemed just right, expressing my new (I thought adult) self perfectly.

David published his first book of poetry (*Night Cries*). I began showing my precious attempts to him and to friends. He liked to guide me along those paths he had already traversed, and I liked to be guided. Though we did spar, especially in and around our advanced poetry class. David had a job by this time — temporary we were sure — editing for a government department, but he decided to audit the class "to keep in touch." There were four women in the class. One wrote descriptions of setting the table or grating cheese. The rest of us, including my colleague at the reading, wrote fashionable poems of a violent and furious tone. When I reread the poems all three of us wrote, they seem a jumble of teeth and nails, wounds, burns, amputations, skulls, bones and gallons of blood, particularly menstrual.

One weak chinned man wrote only detailed descriptions of sexual activities in the tone of one who is sure he is the

*Opposite:*
Henry Kreisel, teacher and writer, at the University of Alberta. Acclaimed author of *The Rich Man* and *The Betrayal*, Kreisel first entered Canada as an Austrian "enemy alien," a member of the post-war internment camps set up in this country by the British.

first to ever try such things. But generally David's poems — which were far more polished than those of anyone else — set the mode for the men. There was more playfulness and humour than in the verse the women wrote, but underneath the same leaden despair prevailed. Horses, chickens, pet and wild dogs, hookers, birds, and foetuses died. Pleasure and morality were illusory and moments of knowledge came only through confrontations with awful nature, going eyeball to eyeball with a grizzly, say, or a raven.

Most of the students in the class were or had been involved with each other and wrote about it, adding a certain tension to the class. When weak chin wrote "Swallow me", we all had a good idea who was being addressed. When a pale, anorexic waif compared herself to a nail about to be clipped, we frowned at the suspected clipper. Of course, we were supposed to speak only of the diction, the rhythm, only of whether the poem in question "worked". But comments from the irritated subject on the validity of the perceptions, on the truth of the poem, did sneak into the discussions.

The professor, youngish though already well known and well published, remained aloof, pretending he didn't notice the subtext. He never suggested that we were disappointing him. He was trying, that year, to write politically engaged work. It was, after all, the late sixties. But not one of us ever tried a verse on Vietnam. "Maybe the problem is in the lyric form," he said once; "its essence is subjectivity."

David and I didn't argue over our writing about each other. What else would we write about? Rather it was what each of us saw as a poaching of perceptions that got us going. I told David about the sensation I experienced each time I drove down a particular stretch of road and passed a deserted phone booth. He used it in his "Ode to River Road." David told me about an evening with his pals that included a tree decapitation and a careless driving charge, and I used that.

"Not that you gave any sense of the exhilaration. You're so controlled."

"Unfair."

"You like it safe. How often have I asked you to move in with me?" David leaned over, pressing his lips into my neck, tickling me with his beard.

"Moderation."

"I know. Balance. Come on. We'll balance. We'll moderate." We were in the front hall, sitting on the steps. "I like it here."

"Don't you like me?" More kisses.

"Umm... as well you know... but I'm not ready."

"You think of the inspiration you'd lose. All that suffering. Look at your Ode, the one in Tamarack."

"But it was your experience of driving home late that I was writing about."

"I'm glad to see you admit it. I'm not the only one stealing ideas."

"We're getting off track here. You know if you moved in with me it would open up a whole new world of responses. Think of the material."

A small, round shadow had appeared at the opaque glass at the top of the door opposite. "Wait. Look."

Opening the door, we found Mimma scrambling down from the top of two chairs she had balanced one on the other.

"I told her she couldn't see through that glass, but she was desperate to find out what you two were up to." Cesare was sitting at the kitchen table eating bread and oil soup. "I would have told her if she wasn't so young."

I settled in the chair beside Cesare. "Don't say anything vulgar. I know you were thinking it. You have that expression. Don't. Soup, David?"

Beginnings and endings, they order and colour our memories. David and I. If I remember from the beginning I recall all the particularities: his widow's peak, his slightly stiff walk, the way his face lit up, the way he turned a phrase, the tone of his voice when he spoke to me, his gentleness that made me feel wrapped up, shielded, safe and separate from the rest of the world. I recall those evenings when we ate and read and loved in his bed, evenings when we seemed to conquer the world and each other from between those slightly worn flannel sheets. If I remember from the beginning, I recall the elation of whizzing down country roads, the joy of drinking and smoking and talking and laughing too much. Much too much. We were young, sensitive, smart, and, best of all, poets. We felt in touch with the truth, even if we thought it consisted of there not being any truth that wasn't relative. We were originals and knew or could know endlessly.

But, if I remember from the end, I recall how the elation could sink down, down into depression, the sense of specialness into paranoia. It was not David's fault. I had been familiar with depression and paranoia since childhood. When his mouth tightened, when he began to ridicule, when he couldn't or wouldn't talk, I provided no balance. We would drop together. His bed became a pit. We lay immobile. To move a hand was difficult. Turning over brought nausea. We had to struggle against the weight of the world to breathe.

Whenever the end began — I could point to one argument or the other or at least the time I bent my head to tongue a baroque path across his bare chest and bent into a cloud of sweet perfume, not mine — I understood that it was the end in a small hotel room in Rome. I had finished my courses for my master's degree in classics that spring and was in Rome to start work on my thesis. Between exams and leaving for Rome, I had gone down to visit my family for three weeks. David had called once and written twice. We discussed my joining him at his parents' cabin for a couple of days as I had other summers. But my parents wanted me to try to influence my sister to give up an unsuitable man. "Besides," they kept saying, "we hardly ever see you." My father asked several times, "what exactly will be you doing in Rome?" After I had explained, he would ask again, "but what is it for? What's the purpose?" He wanted me to succeed as he hadn't. He had immigrated too late in life; his education had counted for nothing here and, besides, he never did learn how to speak English properly. But the country was there for me. "Yours for the taking. . . That's why we came." Going to study old ruins in the old country was a turning away. "You must think of the future." He repeated, "the future."

My mother's practicality flowed in another direction. She was convinced that I was going to be kidnapped for the white slave trade. "Everyone knows about Rome," she would say.

"I'll come to the airport," David had said on the phone. "If you can't come earlier, you can't. But I'll come. We'll hold hands for a couple of hours."

"And smile secret smiles."

"The most secret."

He didn't come. I made my parents leave me at the check-in counter. I positioned myself in a chair close to the glass doors. I waited. I tried to focus my eyes on a paperback but kept looking up, scanning. I moved to a chair by the top of the escalator in case he came up through Departures. I went to buy cigarettes, another magazine. I circled the airlines counter — slowly. I went back to the chair by the escalator and sat in the hard light. At ten minutes to boarding time I phoned the co-op house he had recently moved into. A girl answered. She didn't know where he was, hadn't seen him that day.

"He said he'd meet me here. To say goodbye. I'm going to be away for. . . He said. . . . "

There was a long silence and when she spoke she sounded as if she was speaking to herself. "The bastard. He hasn't said anything."

Although I realized then what I had avoided realizing before, that David had moved in with Miss Perfume, I still hoped. In the airplane, on the bus and, finally, in the *pensione*, I hoped. My will was stretched and taut. The bond could not be broken, not if I held on. For four days I waited in that tiny room with bed, bureau and sink. Of course, I did go out. I cased the neighborhood. I found a cheap *tavola calda*; I started working in the library of the British school. I made notes on file cards in a tiny, controlled script. Yet, what I remember is the waiting. Day and night, I willed him to fly to my side. I willed each step in the hall to be his. "I'm so sorry," he would say, "you see. . . " I willed a phone call. "A mistake." The hall sounds became the chambermaid hurrying to call me. Finally, I willed a letter. Special delivery. I calculated the fastest it could possibly arrive.

And it did arrive. Not when I calculated but soon after. It was full of apologies and explanations (an appointment, an unexpected delay, then a flat tire, with hints of further illumination on his "big mistake".) But it was too late. Not as I had calculated. I had stopped waiting.


When I began university, I was addicted to barbituates. The pills had been prescribed after a breakdown in high school, and after two years of purple pills six times a day to calm me down and big yellow pills twice a day to pep me up, I couldn't do without them. One night, towards the end of my freshman year, I took too many pills. I can't remember the precipitating cause; no doubt, something had happened that resurrected my old sense of unworthiness, something to do with David. I didn't consciously sit down and swallow a bottle of pills. But, during the night, wanting so much to block out the panic, I took an indeterminate number. I passed out in front of my bureau. (I had been staring at myself in the mirror). The crash brought Maria, and her cry, Cesare. He began shouting, they told me later, as soon as he saw me, and it was his furious voice that first penetrated the blackness. I was pulled back to his curses and the acrid smell of my vomit. Maria propped me up, sponged my face, force-fed me coffee, "my sweet poor little baby". Cesare walked me back and forth, back and forth, all the while spitting out obscenities.

The next day he was calm. "I want every one of the pills you have left."

"But I can't. You're crazy. I need them," I said and went on to say many other things about my nerves and my sensitivity and how they misunderstood, it had been an accident, they'd overreacted — they could have let me sleep.

"You've thought too much of yourself. Been allowed to. And all those excuses about your mother and your father and what they did and what they said. Excuses. You chose. And I tell you this: accident or not, you must stop with those pills. . . . We'll see you through."

And they did, through the tears and the shakes, through the nausea and the sleepless nights, with kindness and patience.

I wished for them in the solitude of Rome when day after day passed without my exchanging a personal word with anyone. I wished for Cesare and Maria; I wished for the purple pills; I wished for David. And I could have, would have, none of them. Ever again.

The beginning of loss. I graduated into losses deeper and wider: my idea of myself as a poet, my first baby (stillborn), my first husband. I have written "first", but who knows if I will ever have another? Mathew. I am so ruled by our so recent end that I refuse the thought of new births. It is six months since he left me, six months since he went to "her": six months of recriminations, the legal and the merely verbal. He was false to me, and yes, I to him. When did the falseness, the end, begin? No, it's too close to remember. I cannot sort openings and closings, means and ends. I need simply to mourn, to rage and blame and mourn.

But I'm not alone. I have Jessica and Arthur to sustain, to delight and to exhaust me. I work for the historical sites branch of Alberta Culture and can work on my poems only late at night while the children sleep. I am tired, everyday, tired.

Sometimes, at the supermarket or in the street, I bump into David with his wife and children. He teaches at a college now. He has little time to write but he does what he can. He has a chapbook coming out soon — "I'm going to call it *Adjustments*." Though I'm sure he would no longer define himself as a poet. Like me, he has a boy and a girl. They're almost as gorgeous as mine. Once, at McDonald's, he was without his wife and we decided to share a booth. The kids spilled pop, threw chips and fingerpainted with ketchup.

"I knew you'd make a good father. That first day."

Jon Whyte, Banff poet.

Sam Uhlick, potter, in his Edmonton studio.

Myrna Kostash, author of *All of Baba's Children*, outside her summer home "Tulova," near Two Hills.

Sylvain Voyer, painter.

His laugh was short, ironic, but loud enough to carry over the din. "The only promise I did fulfill."

"Your children are beautiful."

"And yours. Quite amazing."

"Mutual admiration here." His smile still made me lose my train of thought. I wished I hadn't thrown the Don Quixote away.

My end with Plath redefined the beginning. In those years in between, she was an inevitable measuring stick. For "bright" women of my generation she was held up, practically promoted, as role model and warning. And I could see the similarities, especially after the letters and journals were published: over-protective, difficult parent(s), scholarships, sensibility, the thirst for fame and family, love and laurels. But the measuring found me wanting. She had reached the heights: in education, in success, in suffering, and best of all, in embracing death. I was stuck on the ground floor, limited and cautious.

I became aware of the end a couple of months ago at a performance. It was one of two dramatizations of Plath's life at a fringe-theater festival. As usual these days, my time was accounted for, budgeted. I hadn't read any of her work for a long time, hadn't wanted to, but I made an effort to attend at least one, partly in respect to the old allegiance, partly to see what she would say to me now that I was as betrayed, as alone as she had been.

This audience was smaller than the one at that first reading. They were more varied in age and dress though with a preponderance of exercise clothes, and certainly there were more women than men. Edmonton had acquired a veneer of sophistication. Outside, under the striped tents, espresso and Grand Marnier were being served in plastic cups. In the hall, *Sylvia* was sandwiched between two local creations: *The Cosmic Garbage Bin* and *Shit and Death are Everywhere*. The actresses were all young and intense. They rolled out Plath's words with even more relish, if less respect, than that first actress. And the audience wallowed as much as the other, wallowed in the words, wallowed in death, tourists on a dark, dark river.

While I, closer in age and circumstance to Plath on that cold night when she left bread and milk in her infants' room so they wouldn't be hungry when they awoke and she was no longer there, closer in loss to the moment she turned on the gas jets and left those babies forever, I was again embarrassed. This time, instead of the accompanying fascination, there was distaste. She was still a warning but not to the dangers of husband and children.

When did the falseness start? I wanted to say as I stood before that university audience. True art is slow, yes, but how long? Instead I stood, awkward, slightly slumped, my tongue dry. Instead I began to read a poem of graduation.

> Beginning from ends
> Opening and closure. . .

James Agrell-Smith, *Portrait of the Poet*, 1956, woodcut.

# CITY LIFE

Robert Scott, *Composition 86-87*, 1985, acrylic on canvas.

Thomas and Benjamin Fairbrother, Edmonton.

# Excerpts from
## *RIVERDALE POLICE GAZETTE*

by
Allan Shute

### POLICE NAB INDY 500 BOZO

Screaming tires and a roaring engine rudely awakened River-dalians at 3:40 am Tuesday, May 29. Some idiot in a black muscle car held his own personal Indy 500 on our historic streets and avenues for a good ten minutes.

The switchboard at the police station lit up like Colecovision as irate citizens reported this numbskull's brakestands at each point of the compass. (A brakestand involves locking the brakes while the nut behind the wheel depresses the accelerator causing the rear tires to smoke and hop.)

The noise made many people think the car was going to end up in bed with them.

Highlights of the mad run include a brakestand at 90th St & 100th Ave, crossing Rowland Road at 89th St at high speeds without stopping, torquing down an alley east of 88th St past a duplex containing a light-sleeping off-duty police officer, missing by 2 1/2 feet John the Painter's car (see Ads) at 101A Ave and 89th St, and the grand finale in front of a duplex at 10218 - 90th St.

"I looked out the window to see what the noise was," reports Brian Knight of the Riverdale Co-op unit across the street, "and I thought we had fog like last Thursday when I was up to the Sidetrack. I couldn't even see the light pole." The pall of tire smoke was visible from the McFrog Block.

The Historian discovered 1/4" deep tire tracks and fluffy mounds of rubber. Tracks ran the better part of half a block and lurched wildly about, coming within inches of parked vehicles.

A fully-dressed Bill Reid, also of the Co-op unit, was first on the street. He was joined by Jody Bevan, the off-duty policeman, dressed only in jogging pants. Kathy Wheeler, who lives in Brian Knight's old house, noticed a skulking figure behind Mrs. Comin's hedge, and alerted the pair.

A stocky 6'2" fellow smelling of burnt rubber and alcohol came staggering out to join the small crowd. "Shum commotion here tonight!" he reportedly said. He was detained by Jody and Bill who engaged him in conversation.

Two police cars screeched up soon thereafter and hauled the lout away.

A smoking vehicle was located rammed into a bush behind 10220 - 90th St. The tires were still hot fifteen minutes later.

WEATHER: Warmer after cool period.

### PROMINENT PUBLISHER LINKED TO ARSON

Mother's Day in Riverdale was rudely rocked by scandal at 4:54pm when civic authorities learned of a private enterprise attempt at firebuggery on Cameron Avenue — which has a long-standing reputation for unusual behaviour.

A firetruck from the No. 1 Firehall wailed to a stop at the juncture of the alley and Cameron Avenue whereupon the officer in charge inquired at a nearby house surrounded by pink flamingoes . . . presumably to obtain directions. The truck then swooped down one third of a block to the empty lot just below where **Allan Shute**, age 33, lives at **9327 Cameron Avenue**.

Shute was caught red-handed tending an alleged fire with Eddylite matches in his possession. He told the firemen, who used his garden hose to put out the fire, that he had just spent half a day mowing a hillside of City property infested with sow thistle, native grasses and broken beer bottles and had enough crud to fill twenty garbage bags and there was no way he was going to bag it all up just so some garbage truck had to haul it 6 1/2 miles out of town.

"I know what you mean," said the fireman in charge, taking Shute's name and particulars. "It's this pollution control by-law. We got a complaint so here we are."

Later in an exclusive interview with the nosy *Gazette*, Shute described the person who finked on him as "sub-cretinous".

"If you can't tell the difference between a bonfire and a house fire," he said, "you should bloody well dust off your copy of *The Boy Who Called Wolf* and smarten up too."

After several bottles of chilled Pil, Shute admitted he was "unrepentant as hell" and would "do it again" except "the cops got [his] name."

No tickets were issued as it was such a sunny afternoon.

WEATHER: Warmer.

### BELOVED TEACHER PASSES ON

Generations of Riverdale students were saddened to hear of the Jan. 11 death of one of the city's best all-time teachers, **Mrs. Doris Redman**, 69. She taught Grade 2 in Room 2 at Riverdale Elementary for 40 years until her retirement in 1972.

Born July 16, 1909, Mrs Redman played baseball and basketball and organized the Grade 2 boys' soccer team every fall. In the spring, she'd produce the Annual Maypole Festival.

Wayne Gretzky holds aloft the first Stanley Cup to come to Alberta, May 19, 1984.

Above all that, she was an excellent teacher of the old school. **Robert Hunter** of Cameron Avenue, one of her former pupils, describes her as "an acer!"

"She was strict as hell, but the best teacher I ever had! She had a heart of gold and could see good things in each kid, even me! When I went into Grade 3, I really missed her!"

## HOME BIRTH MIRACLE ON 89TH STREET

"A miracle has happened!" Wilfred L. Haight had scarcely debarked the Number 56 before he passed on the good news. "You know my little dog Tippy? She had a puppy!"

Until 3pm January 5th, Mr. Haight hadn't suspected a thing. But he had noticed that Tippy hadn't been jumping up in his lap lately. That afternoon, his dog did jump up into his lap — and had a male baby dog right before his eyes.

When the *Historian* asked after the paternity of the wee pup, Mr. Haight's eyes lit up as he replied, "Black as the ace of spades."

Wilfred Haight is of United Empire Loyalist descent and lives in the historic Gowan House. Ald. Charles Gowan was a City of Edmonton alderman from 1910 to 1912.

So far no name has been given the puppy. Could our readers suggest possible names for our newest 89th Streeter?

## FAREWELL, DUTCH FLATS

By the time you read this, the Dutch Settlement may be little more than a memory. Our friends were originally asked to vacate by the end of 1984, but received an extension to March 31st.

We'll miss their cheery faces and pioneer homes. Farewell **Walter Sowchyn** of Wally's Place. Sowch, as he was called as a child, was born in the same house he lived in.

Farewell, **Del and Karen Affluck**. Thanks for delivering the *Historian* these past few years.

Farewell, **Max**, the large and gentle dog who kept the peace on Waterfront Road.

WEATHER: Better next week.

## LOVERS' LANE ABUSE HARD TO CURB, SAY POLICE

Keeping hookers and their clients out of Riverdale is an uphill battle, say City Police in response to recent news coverage about the problem.

"Unless we catch them in the act," said one spokesman, "we can't charge them with anything. Prostitution itself is not a crime.

Soliciting for business is, but you practically have to see them exchange money to make it stick."

Unless the couple is parked in a park area after eleven o'clock, police cannot force them to move on.

The police regularly patrol the area and check IDs of those they find. "This usually cools their ardor," said one policeman on patrol.

But police don't feel an increase in patrols will solve anything. "If anything, it just gives residents a false sense of security."

Police do not recommend Riverdalians taking personal action because the situation could become dangerous. "You should consider instead increasing the lighting down there."

Despite official caution, one 89 Street resident was successful in curbing hoohah on his front street several years back by snapping flash pictures through the windows and rapping on the windshield with a crowbar.

"It was the same girls coming to the same place, so I just broke that little habit," said the morally outraged vigilante who wished to remain anonymous. "Who wants to find kleenexes and whatnot on your front stoop?"

## $11,000 FOUND NEAR RIVER

Kids pitching rocks into the North Saskatchewan River stumbled upon a massive pile of loot the afternoon of Friday, October 24.

According to scuttlebutt, one lad was searching for another rock to throw when he happened upon the money. Another child, a larger girl, snatched the money away and ran home. The lad ran to the store to call the police.

The money is now with the police who are searching for the owner. Should the money be yours, gentle reader, be sure to provide the police with accurate details and why the money container smelled of marijuana.

If the owner is not found within 90 days the money will be returned to the finder.

And there's never a dull moment in Riverdale.

## IN MEMORIAM *by Ursula O. Ulrich*

On September 8, 1986 in Calgary, **Mrs. Johanne Frida Charlotte Scriba** passed away unexpectedly following a relatively minor surgical intervention to relieve heart troubles.

Mrs. Scriba was born March 5th, 1917 in Hermannsburg (Northwest Germany). Trained as a midwife, she worked as a nurse in the Royal Alex from 1956 (the year she arrived in Canada to wed Johann Scriba) until 1960.

Starting line, Sourdough River Raft Race, Klondike Days, Edmonton.

*Opposite:*
Bike race, Groat Road, Edmonton.

From 1960 to 1966, Johann & Johanne Scriba farmed near Dunstable, Alberta, 50 miles northwest of Riverdale. According to Mr. Scriba, this was the happiest period for his wife in Canada. In 1966, the Scribas returned to live in Riverdale, first as renters in a house on the upper end of Cameron Avenue and then as owners of their own charming little house (reminiscent of Rose Red's overgrown castle) north of Rowland on 89th.

Mrs. Scriba is survived by her husband, Johann, and a sister, who came from Germany to attend the memorial service at St. John's Lutheran Church, and who returned to Germany with Mrs. Scriba's body that was put to its final resting place in the family vault in Hermannsburg.

Although failing health prevented Mrs. Scriba from taking her cherished long walks these last three years, most residents of the North of Rowland Road enclave fondly remember her tall figure moving briskly through Dawson Park.

WEATHER: Sunny but keep your jacket on.

## POLICE FISH FOR HOT CARS

Tight-lipped city detectives, assisted by a skindiver and Cliff's Towing, hauled two stolen cars out of the river on Tuesday, October 14. They left a third in its watery grave because it had sunk too far into the muck.

An appreciative Riverdale crowd gathered at the necking spot on Waterfront Road just south of the Hall where three power poles stand guard. They particularly enjoyed seeing one car break loose and fall back into the river after it had been winched all the way up.

The operation, which spanned several hours, netted a nifty red Olds Cutlass with white racing stripes, and a fully-loaded late-model Thunderbird.

Police are investigating the possibility of a small gang of joyriders who steal cars, race them around town, and then dump them in the same spot. It is not known if the runaway stolen car which exploded at the bottom of Cameron Avenue on Labour Day is connected.

It would be a shame if this gang of louts lived in our neighbourhood or nearby. Unfortunately the evidence points in this direction. Residents are being asked to keep their eyes open.

## BIKING TO WORK IS FASTEST

Commuting to work by bicycle beats taking the bus or your own car. A race organized by Bicycle Commuter president Tooker Gomberg of 28 Sundance proved the point.

Cyclist and Strathcona MLA Gordon Wright took 13 minutes to make the trip from the Energy Conservation Centre on Saskatchewan Drive to City Hall. He beat City Transportation Manager Bob David on No. 132 bus by 30 seconds. John Harms, chairman of the Alberta Motor Association, happened by 10 minutes later.

David pointed out that he sat warm and dry in the bus reading while Wright huffed and puffed in the rain, and had to walk his bike up the stairs beneath the Mac.

Gomberg, who had C. Roy Tailor sew a ritzy cover to his bike helmet, staged the event to publicize Bike Ahead Week.

No stranger to cyclist activism, Gomberg hails from Montreal where he led a series of public protests in the mid-70s which led to bicycles being allowed on the subway. One event included an attempt, in full media glare, to part the waters of the St. Lawrence to allow cyclists to cross.

Another ploy was the carry-on campaign. As it was legal to transport anything other than bikes on the subway, Tooker and fellow bike nuts carted on ladders, wheelbarrows, ironing boards and the like. They even took a person dressed up as an elephant to the office of the transit commission head.

Today cyclists are welcome on the subway.

WEATHER: Prepare for rush of ecstasy.

Gail Greenough, 1986 World Show Jumping Champion, on Mr. T.

# Excerpts from
## *THE EYE OPENER*

### by
### Bob Edwards

The late Paddy Nolan used to tell this story about a man whom he had just got off on a charge of horse stealing:

"Honor bright now, Bill, you did steal that horse, didn't you?"

"Now look here, Mr. Nolan," was the reply, "I always did think I stole that horse, but since I heard your speech to that 'ere jury, I'll be doggoned if I ain't got my doubts about it."

☆

With all due respect to the memory of the late "Judge" Travis of Calgary, we have often wondered what that man got out of life. When he died Judge Travis was a very old man and had just reached the million mark. In spite of which he was up to his neck in real estate deals and busy from morning till night raising his rents and engaging in altercations with the assessor. The paralytic seizure which carried him off occurred in a real estate office where he was fixing up a deal.

☆

Society Note:

Lt. Col. James Walker is in the city today having been here for the last thirty years. He will likely be here tomorrow also, and the day after.

☆

One of the saddest cases of suicide within our recollection occurred last Sunday evening when James L. Cameron, an old friend of ours and for years a respected citizen of Calgary, hanged himself from a tree near the south end of the C. & E. railway bridge. Mr. Cameron was around his usual haunts Saturday and appeared well and hearty. He was naturally of a jocular turn and had many friends. His untimely death will be widely mourned.

His body swaying in the early morning breeze was discovered on the Monday by the crew and passengers of the Calgary and Edmonton northbound. The train was brought to a standstill and the conductor, followed by a number of passengers, hastened to the scene and had the body borne on a handcar to the station, whence it was removed to Shaver's Undertaking Parlors for the inquest. The news quickly spread over the city and the members of the lodge to which the deceased belonged took charge of the remains and undertook arrangements for a suitable funeral.

Coroner Costello summoned a jury, of which Alderman T. A. P. Frost was foreman, and a rigid inquiry was instituted as to the causes leading up to the act of self-destruction. Several witnesses were called who testified that the deceased was a bachelor in good circumstances, living in an apartment block with little or no worldly cares or worries. He was a man of cheerful disposition and was known to be kind to his mother, who resided in Brockville, Ont. A letter found on his person, addressed to the coroner, was finally opened in the presence of the jury and partly explained the rash act. It read as follows:

Dear Sir — This letter will be found on my person and should reach you in due course. I am taking my own life, not in a moment of passing insanity, but in a fit of terrible depression. My naturally cheerful temperament precludes any idea of degenerate mentality, my mind as a general rule being absolutely normal. So pray direct the jury not to return a verdict of suicide while temporarily insane. No man is saner than I.

Today is Sunday. When I arose this morning the Salvation Army band was passing my windows playing a frightful tune. This was a bad start. The Hudson's Bay restaurant, where I usually feed, was closed, and I partook of an exceedingly bum breakfast at a joint on Ninth Avenue and was overcharged by the waitress. On returning to my rooms I found I had nothing to read, so went out again to buy some papers and magazines. The hotel book stores were shut down tighter than Billy be damned. I then decided to get a box of cigars and pass the day in calm reflection and quiet contemplation. The cigar stands were also closed.

Returning to my rooms I took a seat by the window and watched the dreary groups of men who gathered on the street

Saddledome, Calgary

Heritage Days

corners and huddled in doorways with nothing to do and nowhere to go. Pretty soon the church bells began to ring and I beheld a man who had flimflammed me out of $500 the previous day walking down the street with an immense Bible under his arm. A feeling of intense irritation came over me, and I felt in all my pockets for a cigar to sooth my feelings. Nothing doing. I then put on a hat and sallied forth to see if the drug stores were open. Perhaps here, I thought, might be found some relief in the cigar line and peradventure the obliging clerk might even be worked for a glass of spiritus fermenti. Vain hope! The obliging clerk explained that while he was distressed beyond measure that he could not accommodate me with either of these commodities, he would be delighted to let me have as much calomel and Seidlitz powders as I wanted. He said he had a fine lot of those delicacies. I then decided to take a brisk walk. No sooner had I made a fair start than I ran into a flock of people, all dressed in black and looking very lugubrious, on their way to church. I crossed the street and ran into another bunch. Turning down an alley I regained my rooms by a circuitous route and decided to go to bed. When half undressed I changed my mind and reclothed myself. It then occurred to me that a bachelor friend who had rooms on the same flat might possibly have a bottle of beer to spare, or perhaps a shot of booze. This man usually keeps a small assortment for emergencies. But when I entered his room he was fast asleep in bed and when I woke him up the first words he uttered were, "Say you haven't got such a thing as a drop of whiskey, or a bottle of beer? I had a thick night last night." So that settled that.

The Salvation Army again passed my windows, the drum making a most diabolical noise and the trombone going oompa-oompa in great style. Once more I put on my hat and sallied forth. Groups of homeless men were collected in the entrances of moving picture palaces, looking at the gaudy pictures of the films to be put on the following day. What struck me more than anything else was the absence on the street of any one I knew. None of my social or business acquaintances were to be seen. They were no doubt comfortably ensconced in their cosy homes in the bosom of their families, or what is more likely, were playing billiards and quaffing goblets of Scotch and Polly at the club. Not being a club man, I felt lost indeed.

Lunch time came around and I entered another Ninth Avenue joint and downed a cup of unspeakable coffee and a chunk of apple pie with leather underpinning. On my way back I ran into the black-robed crowd returning from church, some of whom I knew and had to bow to. One man in particular I tried to stop, because I knew that he seldom, if ever, was without a flask in his hip pocket, but his wife was with him and he passed on. Ships that pass in the night.

A furtive visit to the various hotels produced nothing but disappointment. The proprietors, most of whom I knew, were all out driving in their automobiles, the outward and visible result of 15 cent beer, and I did not happen to know any of the clerks. At any rate, they all said the same thing, that "they didn't have the key."

The gloom deepened. A man for whom I have an intense dislike, and whom I knew but slightly, stopped me on the street and began explaining to me why Billy Manarey should be elected commissioner. That settled it. This was the last straw. I decided to go to some remote spot and in the cool shades of the evening end it all. Hell were a paradise to such a Calgary Sunday. True, Monday is tomorrow, but Sunday will come around again and I dread to face it. I am not a coward.

What man dare, I dare:
Approach thou like the rugged Russian Bear,
The arm'd rhinoceros, or the Hyrcan tiger;
Take any shape but an Ontario Sunday,
And my firm nerves shall never tremble.
Unreal mockery, hence!

In my rooms I found a suitable length of rope, such as had enwrapped my trunks on many a well-remembered holiday, and wound it around the belt inside my coat. Then I sat down to pen this letter, my last farewell to the world. It will be found in my pocket. My affairs are in good shape and I am addressing a letter to my banker to act as my executor and devote the whole of my current account to the poor. This should buy at least three turkeys. Goodbye. Tell the Rev. Marshall and his co-stiffs that my blood is on their heads.
Sadly yours,
JAMES L. CAMERON

After a brief consultation the jury returned a verdict of "Death due to neurotic effect of a Calgary Sunday," with a rider to the effect that Calgary Sundays should be modified in their severity. The coroner agreed with the verdict and invited the jury out to have a drink. The funeral was largely attended and many wreaths were placed on the coffin as a tribute of affection and esteem. A message of condolence was forwarded to the sorrowing mother in Ontario, who, it is said, is prepared to bring an action for heavy damages against the Rev. Marshall and his co-stiffs.

☆

The scenery round Edmonton is lovely. It doubtless inspired the bard who sang "Ye Banks and Braes of Bonny Rat Creek." The view from the Edmonton Club is superb, looking down the valley of the Saskatchewan on to the dilapidated gold dredges and battered grizzlies of days that are no more. After a few horns inside, the gorgeousness of the scene becomes more and more impressive. It looks especially fine after two stiff Collinses.

☆

The millennium has came.

The cities of Edmonton and Strathcona are going to celebrate Coronation Day by amalgamating the two municipalities and uniting under the name of "Edmonton." This happy union means that Edmonton will have three breweries instead of only two as heretofore. In breweries she will lead Calgary by one.

☆

Edmonton now estimates that it has a population of over 4,000. Estimates are easy to make. Calgary with her bona fide population of 11,000 is seriously thinking of estimating her population at 25,000 just to prove that its imagination is not inferior to Edmonton's.

☆

We hate to say anything about it, we do for a fact, but how in thunder did the new city hall of Calgary come to cost $350,000 when Pat Burn's splendid residence, which everybody knows well by sight, was erected for less than $25,000? This is a profound mystery — one of the seven mysteries of the world, in fact.

☆

The first thing a man with a new automobile runs into is debt.

☆

When the train pulled into Hamilton, Ont., a passenger put his head out of the window and asked a native:

"My friend, what is the name of this dismal, dried-up, heaven forsaken hole?"

"That's near enough," answered the dejected native. "That's near enough. Let her go at that."

☆

Yes, house-hunting in Calgary is some job. It seems to have driven some people to adopt desperate measures.

Mr. Bott was wending his way home after a tiring day, house-hunting with no result. Passing by the river he heard a splash. Horrors! There was a man struggling in the water. Could it be? Yes — it was his friend Mr. Jopkins. Disregarding his appeals for help, Bott made a rush up town for Jopkins' house agent.

"Excuse me," he said, breathlessly, "but can I have Jopkins' house? He has fallen in the river and is drowning."

"Sorry," said the house merchant, "but you're too late. I've already let it to the man who pushed him in."

☆

That was a wise guy who said that a lawyer is a man who gets two men to strip for a fight and then runs off with their clothes.

☆

"Did you ever hear," began Dave McDougall, the Calgary oldtimer, "about the winter I put in my ranch near Morley in '67? It was what a man might be excused for calling some winter. That is to say, it was cold.

"We began to notice unusual symptoms along in November. To begin with, the creeks all froze solid — clear to the bottom, you understand — and instead of water flowing along in the creek beds there was ice moving along about the same speed. Regular glaciers.

"The creeks where I was emptied into the Bow and of course the Bow was as full as the creeks. So there was nothing left for the creek ice to do but hump up when it reached the river and double back on itself. Then when it got back to head-quarters it had to double up again and go down to the river.

"All the creeks kept up this process until they piled on top of themselves four or five times, or even more than that. Calgary folk looking west thought that the mountains were walking into town. They did, for a fact! We had to tunnel through those creeks to get from one place to another. And we had to keep making new tunnels, too, as the old tunnels kept moving up above our reach, where we couldn't get at 'em. You never saw anything like it, believe me!

"But the worst was yet to come. The first cold snap lasted until along in January. Then we had the usual January thaw. But this thaw hadn't got good and started when a big freeze set in one night and froze the ground so quick and so hard that it popped the rabbits and the gophers up out of their holes the way a little boy pops a pea out of its pod. I tell you it was a corker."

"It must have been," said J. J. McHugh, regarding the speaker darkly.

"You bet it was," said Dave. "Every one of those rabbits and gophers just stayed there in the air — frozen stiff, some of them six or eight feet above the ground. There were so many of them that a man couldn't go out without bumping his head. It was much like walking in a dense forest, only the animals were closer to our heads than the branches of the trees would have been."

"Certainly," said Colonel Walker, with a strained look.

"The only way we could get a glimpse of the sun was to take an ice axe and climb up the side of one of the creeks. I never expect to see the like again."

"It must have been bally cold," ventured an Englishman.

"It was," said Dave.

"Well," put in J. J., "I suppose that when you wanted dinner all you had to do was go out and build a fire anywhere and the dinner would thaw out of the air and fall down into the pot, eh?"

"Not on your life! It was so cold that whenever anybody tried to start a fire the air melted and put the fire out. Every time. But that's not all —,"

"Oh, yes it is!" cried J. J., as he and the colonel reached for their hats and hastened over to the Alberta.

The Englishman remained behind. When he showed up at the Alberta an hour later, he looked pale and his eyes were popping out of his head.

"Make mine fairly strong," said he to the bartender.

# Excerpts from
# *SATURDAY AND SUNDAY*

by
Edmund Kemper Broadus

There is nothing distinctive about it. If you were bowling past it on the winding river-driveway you would get a fleeting impression of a bungalow, with brown shingled roof and brown shingled walls, with open porches two-thirds surrounding it. In winter you would see, through a tracery of bare branches, Little Brown House lifting from a smooth expanse of glistening snow. In summer, you would apprehend it as mere bits of brown wall and white wood-work, bowered in foliage of blue spruce and birch and Russian poplar and Manitoba maple, with honeysuckle bushes half concealing the porches. In front, on the other side of the driveway, you would see a wooded slope, dropping sharply down to the river bed of the Saskatchewan, with the valley, visible for miles in the clear air, marking out a great V, above the point of which you stand.

For two expatriates from a warmer climate, Little Brown House was the fruition of lessons learned in a hard school. Edmonton was a century old as a Hudson's Bay post when we came to it, but as a city it was in the mushroom stage. Houses were built with careless haste, and a perfect genius for producing pretentious "effects" with cheap materials. Our first two winters in a rented house were a medley of chronically frozen pipes and rooms too arctic to be usable for six months of the year. We joked about it — but also we swore an oath that some day we should be warm in latitude 54, though we lived in a stoke-hole to accomplish it.

And then, one day, we happened to wander to the point of the V overlooking the Saskatchewan — and here forthwith Little Brown House cried unto us to give it being. The city had not reached out even a tentacle to it then. From the brow of the steep wooded valley, the untrodden snow stretched back to a low swell, on the crest of which was a little log cabin, with a log barn beside it. The father of the farmer who lived there had homesteaded it thirty years before, when the nearest railway station was Winnipeg, a trifle over eight hundred miles away. From the pioneer's son, himself no mean adventurer in the wild, we bought a little plot of ground, and then besought, from all and sundry, advice on the vital topic of how to keep warm at "forty below". Our own knowledge of building specifications was limited to a memory, albeit vague, of one who had built an ark of gopher-wood, had made rooms in it, had set a door in the side thereof, and had pitched it within

and without with pitch. Gophers we had in abundance, but no gopher-wood. We thought we should need rooms, and perhaps also a window "in a cubit finished above". But of one thing we were sure — pitched within and without with pitch it must be — or whatever might be the equivalent in a sub-arctic climate. Building-paper, then, of thickest hair-felt, clothed our wooden frame, as with a perennial coat of fur. Within, every room abutted upon a central chimney of many flues, so that the radiation from the bricks should supplement the piped warmth of the furnace. The chimney, I remember, was built before even the foundations were raised, and was completed even to the brick-arched fire-places. There, for many days, it remained, baring its domestic hearthstones to the middle air, till the slow carpenters came to lift the structure round it, to swathe the frame in that quintessential fur coat, and to apply the epidermis of shingles. And, the next winter, through double windows almost opaque with frost, we peered out, content and warm, upon a frozen world.

"Forty below!" It seems to be a sort of shibboleth among those who dwell south of the International Boundary, for the terrors of a northern winter. "What do you wear?" "How can you *live*?" "What can you *do*?" — asks the casual inquirer. But after all, when you have learned how to deal with it, forty below (I have seen it sixty, but fifteen or twenty degrees more or less after you get that far don't really matter, and forty will do for a standard) — after all, forty below is not a terrible thing. It spells beauty, a beauty austere and magnificent.

With us, the winter comes early. About August twenty-fifth, there will probably be a touch of frost. As we slip into September, the days remain hot — intensely hot sometimes — but the nights grow steadily colder, and frosts become a commonplace. As September draws to a close the leaves either gradually drop from the trees, or (more often) are suddenly bitten off over night, by a severer frost, and you wake up next morning to find only

"Bare ruin'd choirs, where late the sweet birds sang."

By October, the fields are sere, the trees have shed all their shrivelled leaves, wild geese honk overhead on their long southward journey, and the ground begins to harden with a

Ukrainian Historical Village.

premonition of that iron frozenness which will reach five feet beneath the surface by mid-winter. The first snow-fall will have come by now; and unless some exceptional mid-winter thaw should occur, you may count on having every dry hard little flake that falls to the ground as your companion until the spring. Harder and more deeply hard grows the ground as November passes, and between the fifteenth and the thirtieth of this month the river, that had rolled its muddy torrent down one long arm of the V toward Little Brown House and had bent sharply back to its recession along the other arm, solidifies into apparently indestructible ice. Soon the steel-blue of the ice gives place to the white glitter of snow, and the broad sinuous ribbon of the river becomes a highway. With the advent of December, Winter hesitates and seems almost to relent. The days are at their shortest, with the sun rising at nine and setting at four, but there is a brief space of warmer weather. The dry, hard snow softens a little, and sometimes even indulges in a tentative thaw; you revel in the untrammelled freedom of temperate days. And then come January and February (twin monarchs of the frost) and with them — forty below!

Even then it is not persistent. I have seen it fluctuate around that temperature for six weeks at a stretch; but ordinarily it will come in short sharp attacks, with restful softenings between. A premonitory snow-fall — and then during the ensuing night the timbers of Little Brown House will begin to sigh and groan, as if some invisible hand were pushing and readjusting the beams. You do not need to look at the thermometer outside to know what is going on. The temperature is dropping, dropping. Next morning, you will look out upon a world, sunlit, frozen, silent. You will go out into it, of course. No one would wish to be immured from that dry, sharp, tonic air. If you are a novice, you will clothe yourself in a heavy fur coat. If you have learned of experience, you will substitute for the fur coat a lighter woollen garment. You will see to it that a fur cap comes well down over your ears, and that you are shod either with moccasins or with loose shoes of soft felt. As you tread upon the wooden side-walk, it cracks like a pistol-shot. You meet another pedestrian, and perhaps, though you may not be ten minutes from home, he will stop you and tell you that your nose is frozen. You rub it sharply with snow, and go on your way rejoicing. You have been initiated into "forty below". As you progress from the suburbs into the city streets, you find yourself scanning every passing nose with humorous intentness. Ah, there is the tell-tale white spot at last. You halt

Mud Racer, Pincher Creek.

October 19, 1986, Eskimo-Stampeder Game, Commonwealth
Stadium, Edmonton.

him and fraternally repay your debt. Teams strain past, hauling heavy loads of coal. Sweat has frozen on the horses; they are white from head to tail. Meanwhile, from every chimney, smoke rises, columnar, unwavering, into the windless air. You are lured back into the open spaces where the white quiet is. Down in the valley, across the river, men are cutting the dead wood and stunted poplars to open a street, and at intervals of a hundred yards have piled their cuttings and lighted them. The axe-strokes are too far away to be audible. Out of the silence the smoke-columns tower toward the sky, regular as a company in open marching order, — the giant body-guard of King Winter, watching over a subjugated world.

And then, mayhap, when night falls, the Aurora will come. Dim narrow spindrifts of light, with blurred edges, stretch across the sky. Imperceptibly they gather and gather, a streamer here, a patch of light there, from the whole northern sphere, making toward the zenith. The scattered streams and zones converge, combine, and long slender arrows of sharper light strike through them, radiating like the spokes of a wheel from zenith to horizon, and turning the arch of heaven into a gigantic cone, whose tapering point seems to have attained an infinite remoteness. And this point, this zenith, becomes suddenly a glory of living light. Masses of pink and green dissolve, resolve, blend, are flung like shimmering veils far down the horizon, and vanish only to reappear with added glory at the zenith. There is no rest to this mad dance of colour. Now it is flung out in nebulous masses, now shot forth in needle-like rays. Slowly the glory fades. The masses at the zenith break into luminous wisps, drift horizon-ward and disappear. And two expatriates, who have braved forty below to stand out in the open and watch the hour's pageant, slip back into the cheerful warmth of Little Brown House once more, while one quotes:

"What, you are stepping westward? Yea, 'Twould be a wildish destiny,
If we, who thus together roam,
In a strange land and far from home,
Were in this place the guests of chance:
Yet who would stop or fear to advance,
Though home or shelter he had non,
With such a sky to lead him on."

# Excerpt from
# THE ANTE-ROOM

## by
## Lovat Dickson

Broadus was a legendary figure in that small upland world. He had been teaching at Harvard when a tubercular gland in his neck put him in a sanatorium. That was in 1909, just at the time when Dr. Tory, the newly-appointed president of Alberta University, was recruiting his first staff from the universities on the coast. Broadus was told that he must live in the West; Tory was advertising for teachers for his foundling. They met; they took to each other. Harvard, where Broadus had taught, and Radcliffe, where Mrs. Broadus had been teaching, were left behind. Edmonton, to the Boston of that time, was almost as remote as the Yukon, and Broadus must indeed have been a dying man, in the eyes of his Cambridge friends, if the demands of his health could drive him to take up a teaching post in a university sprung out of the great plains where but a few years before buffaloes and Indians had roamed, and the Mountie had dispensed law and made order prevail. The banks of the Saskatchewan seemed very far away from Boston Common and the Faculty Club.

English 2, where I first came into contact with this great man, was compulsory for all second-year people proceeding to an Arts Degree, and was a hazardous course designed wickedly by Broadus to trap the worthy into specialization in English, and to undermine, destroy and overwhelm those who took the subject lightly.

He quickly pounced on my pretensions. When our first themes were returned with his markings, I saw to my absolute amazement that I had failed. I thought there must have been some mistake. I folded back the foolscap pages, certain that I would find that there had been an error; he must have mixed my work with that of someone else.

But there was no mistake. Shame, oh, burning shame! Some of my finest phrases were heavily underscored; the sentiments they expressed ridiculed in the margins. The construction of some of my sentences was shown to be faulty, and the verbosity and fulsomeness of my style laid bare with a prick of his waspish pen. I could have wept with embarrassment and injured pride. This was the best I could do, and he could only scoff at it. I began to hate him, and I longed to get even with him, and I ended up by going to his room in the Arts Building that afternoon to argue it out with him.

He was a little man with a large and rather fine head which perpetually shook and trembled like a flower on a long stalk. He wore gold-rimmed spectacles from behind which his eyes looked coldly. He smoked without ceasing, when one cigarette was nearly done stubbing it out with his brown wooden holder, and replacing it with a new one.

He wasted little time with me over the preliminaries.

'I don't know who you are,' he said. 'You've told me your name, but it means nothing to me, and will continue to mean nothing until you can distinguish yourself in some way. Your essay was one of the worst in the whole class. I can understand the son of an immigrant Lithuanian farmer finding difficulty with the English language, but you are Canadian or British and this is your native tongue, and you've abused it more in these few pages than any of these ignorant youths who have been speaking it for a few years.

'Who in God's name told you that you can write? I can see that somebody has flattered you in that way. Well, let me tell you plainly that you can't, and you will fail this course unless you recognize that fact and cease to show off about something for which you haven't the slightest skill.

'I don't want any excuses or explanations. If I have to mark that revolting, nauseatingly pompous essay of yours again, I will mark it even harder. Go away. Depart. Avaunt. Get out of my sight, man, until you can hold your head up and look me in the eye, and say "I have really tried". Goodbye.'

The next I knew, I was out in the hall, my cheeks burning, my mind blazing, not with anger but with a strange kind of excitement. I was determined to show this old man that I was no ordinary undergraduate. After all, I had edited a paper. I had since then contributed a full-page article to the *Edmonton Journal* in commemoration of the shooting of Edith Cavell. He might not think much of my style, but I could earn a living with it. It might not do for English 2, but it did for the *Edmonton Journal*. I would show him.

Ever busy with my pen — my poor pen, held now in such scorn — I had been amusing myself during the summer at Jasper with writing parodies of well-known poems. The fun this exercise offered me was in the contrast it provided between the mellowness of the original and the harsh reality of the matter if a local subject were substituted. I had collected a number of these, and I now interspersed them with some comments after the style of 'Charivaria' in *Punch*, and had sent them off to Mr. Morrison, the editor of the *Edmonton Journal*. He had used them, setting them out in a column on the editorial page where they looked quite neat and important. He asked me for more, and I warmed to my task. Soon I was providing the *Edmonton Journal* with two and sometimes three full columns a week under the heading 'Hodge-Podge'. I got a good deal of fun out of it and quite a lot of money, but Professor Broadus did not seem to notice that he had a real live author in his English 2 class.

What Broadus did notice was that in the essays I was writing for him, I had ceased to show off. The shock treatment had done me good. My style was now so bare it was nearly indecent, and to hide its nakedness I had to cover it with some facts. Broadus called me to his room, and gave me back an essay bearing rather a high mark. The stony quality of his eyes moistened and softened just for the briefest moment before his head shook everything back into firmness again. 'Come to tea,' he said. 'Come and meet my wife. Call for me at 4.15 this afternoon.'

Not, 'I hope you are free', or 'Would you like to come?' Just a command to be there, and I shivered with satisfaction.

It was November, and the first snow had fallen. It lay like icing on a cake, very white where nothing had touched it, yellow and mud-stained where it had fallen into the ruts of car or sleigh tracks. I accompanied the Professor from his office to the car park. In 1924, cars were still comparatively rare around the university. The Professor's was a Star, 1919 model. Its bonnet was swathed in blankets. Raised high on its little tyres, which were festooned with chains, it looked very leggy and rather plucky. The Professor removed the blankets and stuffed them inside, and then adjusted the spark and the gas levers on the steering-wheel, rubbed his hands together briskly, looked at the starting-handle and looked at me. 'Let me do it,' I said, and he made no difficulty, motioning me with his hand to wait while he adjusted himself in the driver's seat. Then I turned the handle, rocking the little car as I did so, until suddenly it caught fire, gave a tremendous shudder, an ear-splitting single pop from its exhaust, and then reverberated and thundered into roaring life. The Professor beamed at me and opened the door for me to get in beside him, and with a jerk we ran crisply over the snow, heading south along the bank of the river.

'I call him Hotspur,' explained the Professor, and quoted beautifully:

'By heaven, methinks it were an easy leap
To pluck bright honour from the pale-faced moon,
Or drive into the bottom of the deep,

Where fathom-line could never touch the ground,
And pluck up drownéd honour by the locks.'

Hotspur, breasting the snowy road, swam with a swan-like motion along the bank above the river. I marvelled that the Professor could find his way, for out there the snow surface was unmarked by any tracks, and perilously close at our right hand the chasm opened, at the foot of which, sixty or seventy feet below, lay the river, already frozen at its sides. The icy wind whistled through the curtains, but we were happy and relaxed, the day's toil being behind us, and tea and the fireside ahead. I was warmed by a glow of purest friendship for this old man. He had done little except insult me since we had first met, but I somehow knew that afternoon as we swayed, slid and ground our way along the snowy road in gallant Hotspur, that he was going to have a profound and exciting influence on my life. Taking care that he should not observe me, I smiled at him.

The house which Broadus had built was an attractive small one, commanding a lovely view across the river valley. It was totally isolated, even in the summer, and no one ever came to do the rough work. Mrs. Broadus, a lady of exceptional beauty and fine breeding, did all.

She came to greet us as we stamped our way into the lamplit house. I had not met a lady for a very long time; she stood, as my mother would have stood, silent and still, and so gracefully, like a figure from a good painting. Her eyes were like my mother's, not the same colour, but large and deep and understanding. Her voice was low like my mother's. I had forgotten. I was suddenly shy and tongue-tied. My heart raced, and I trembled. I was so afraid of looking a fool.

Broadus took me up to his study while she went to the kitchen to get tea. Lamps were lit, and the fire was burning. I saw bookshelves on four sides of the room reaching to the ceiling, but still these could not contain all the books. By his chair was a pile as high as the arm. By hers there was a footstool, and a piece of knitting, with the needles still in it, lay where she had put it down at our coming.

What was it? Where had I been? This book-lined room, the knitting on the footstool, the hissing fire, the Professor's voice going on and on. . . . I had been asleep, I had been having a horrible nightmare. The terrible things I had done since that day we walked away from the cemetery, the emptiness, the growing pains of remorse, the waste, the hopelessness, the despair, and more than anything, the lack of love, the being alone: all this was vanishing, and I hardly dared to speak in case the sound of my voice summoned it all back again.

I had the grace to rise when Mrs. Broadus came in bearing a heavy tray, but I was too gauche to take it from her until the Professor, making ineffectual fumbling to clear the table that stood before the fire, commanded me in tones of thunder to do it. Soon we were seated round the table, and the spirit-lamp was burning under the silver kettle, and there on a plate were scones like those which Keno used to make. And the thinnest bread and butter. And crab-apple jelly. And an uncut fruit cake. I had not sat down to such a tea since I was a child; for years I had not sat down to tea at all. It was a forgotten pleasure.

I was too self-conscious to make the sort of meal my hungry stomach craved for. The Professor masticated, champed and chawed with great deliberation while Mrs. Broadus sat with a slight smile on her lovely face and drew me out. I had resented Mrs. Elliott's vulgar curiosity, and I had always thought it right to keep my story to myself, but before I knew where I was I was telling this lady all. Well, nearly all. She did not say 'Poor boy,' as Mrs. Elliott had done. She looked at me with amusement and said, 'You have been busy,' and the Professor, finishing his splendid tea at this point, dabbed at his lips with his handkerchief and said, 'Too busy to learn some of the elementary facts of our literature.' He smiled at me to show that this was not offensively meant.

'There are half a dozen young men and women in this class who have an ear for the beauty of language, but there isn't one who has been taught to use it. Is there no home in which books are read any more, just for sheer pleasure?'

He was not asking me the question. He had, even to me, the air of a man indulging himself in a pet irritation.

'Read us something then, dear,' said Mrs. Broadus.

'What shall it be, love?' said the Professor, rising and running his fingers lovingly along the shelves.

'Tonight — Hardy. Don't you agree, Mr. Dickson?'

The Professor withdrew a book and settled himself, head shaking furiously under the lamplight. There was a moment's silence, and then his voice came, and my heart responded, hammering against my windpipe so that for a moment I could hardly breathe:

'When the Present has latched its postern behind my
    tremulous stay,
And the May month flaps its glad green leaves like wings,
Delicate-filmed as new-spun silk, will the neighbours say,
"He was a man who used to notice such things"?'

He read on, and between poems talked about the authors. I leant back in my chair, and shut my eyes against the fire and the light of the room, and listened to this wonderful voice making this beautiful music. It was not until it was over, and I was walking back to the university in the darkness, that I remembered the poetry recitations of my youngest years. What foolish amateurs we had been, what nonsense we had declaimed. It shamed me to think that evening after evening we had sung sentimental songs at the piano, and recited Shelley and Byron. We had never read poetry like this. I had never guessed what music our language could make until I had heard it read aloud that afternoon. It was the sound that gripped me, not the sense of the words. That was to come as I made my way forward with painful slowness from the position I had just won.

Manwoman, *Dragon Dance*, n.d., woodcut.

# THE SPIRIT

## The Work of Orest Semchishen

Ukrainian Greek Catholic Church, Craigend, south of Lac La Biche.

Reverend Seraphin Filminoff at prayer before his midday meal, Northville monastery, near Wildwood.

The baking of communion bread. Reverend Filminoff lives in a makeshift "skete" or monastery adapted from an old sawmill near Northville. His life as a monk stresses work, reflection, and prayer.

Reverend Filminoff's sewing machine and vestments. His congregation is a splinter group of the Russian Orthodox Church, a faith in exile from the communism of the Soviet Union.

*Opposite:*
Detail, St. Vladimir's Ukrainian Greek Orthodox Church, Vegreville.

Communion.

Mrs. Wyandy, west of Edson, 1980.

Harvey Wyandy, the son of Mrs. Wyandy.

*Opposite:*
John Diduck, Mundare, 1974.

Felix Plante, 87, carves a wooden cross to mark his wife's grave.

Mannville.

# THE RITES OF SPRING

Sylvain Voyer, *Mrs. Voyer's Backyard*, 1976, acrylic.

Lewis Thomas in his garden at Kapasiwin on Lake Wabamun.

# GARDENING IN ALBERTA

by
Lewis G. Thomas

My apprenticeship in the making of gardens in Alberta was served at Millarville, a rural neighbourhood in the foothills southwest of Calgary. There, along Sheep Creek and its north and south forks, a group of relatively well off settlers from the United Kingdom established themselves a century ago and continued, in the next thirty years, to maintain, with their church, their tennis courts, their polo ground, and their race track, a way of life that recalled a gentler tradition than that of the cowboy and Indian.

Of that tradition the making of gardens was a part and when my parents returned to Sheep Creek and in 1910 settled into a small stock farm, called Cottonwoods Ranch, lying not far below the forks, one of their first preoccupations was to lay out a garden, something that age and infirmity had precluded for the original owners. Seventy-five years later my sister still maintains that garden, enlarged and matured, but still reflecting the images of an English cottage garden translated into forms consonant with the foothills of the Rockies.

The gardener should be at home in almost any environment. He looks at it and his immediate response is to wonder how he can grow things in it. I am using the personal pronoun "he" in its most general sense, as gardening is, or ought to be, the least chauvinist of occupations. Plants, however, have their own ideas about environment and, immediately he puts spade to earth, the gardener must take their needs and preferences into consideration. This immediately involves him in problems of design. The garden is, and this the gardener must face, imposed upon the environment. If the gardener is sensitive to the environment, he will attempt so to design his garden that it will at least be in harmony with its natural surroundings, and not a raw wound forced upon them.

The garden is, by definition, an interference with the natural landscape. It is also a means by which man can mitigate the inevitable consequences of his presence in that landscape. It can certainly deepen and intensify his enjoyment of his surroundings. The garden thus serves to reconcile him to aspects of an environment that at first glance may seem beyond the limits of the tolerable. If the garden is to achieve these goals, it must be in harmony with the natural landscape and, as far as possible, with man's other intrusions upon it. The latter consideration is, admittedly, the more difficult to achieve. Taken together these are the collective principles that govern the design of the well-mannered garden.

The ornamental garden has long preoccupied the settler in

Alberta. The first flower garden there to be noticed in print was Father Lacombe's at Lac St. Anne, praised by Lord Southesk in his book of 1875, as a "... well kept garden, gay with flowers — (some of them the commonest flowers of the woods and plains, brought to perfection by care and labour)." Soon afterwards Canon William Newton, the first Anglican missionary at Edmonton, began to establish his garden at The Hermitage where, a hundred years later, the lilacs he planted still survived. R. Burton Dean, during his thirty-one years in the Mounted Police, made efforts at horticultural embellishment at the posts at which he served. Two books by Annora Brown, a daughter of the Force, evoke an artist's response to the Alberta landscape and *Sketches from Life* has a sensitive and perceptive foreword by the Honourable Frank Lynch-Staunton, Lieutenant Governor of Alberta. Mrs. C. Lynch-Staunton of Pincher Creek compiled one of the earliest Alberta local histories and tradition survives that the sod roof of the Lynch-Stauntons' ranch house burst into bloom with the first spring rains. The Honourable Irene Parlby, Alberta's first woman cabinet minister, made gardens at or near Alix, maintaining her interest in horticulture to the end of her long, busy and fruitful life.

All these gardens represented the individual gardener's adaptation to the exigencies of Alberta's topography and climate. Though my sister's garden at Cottonwoods lies in a relatively sheltered valley, and is today protected by the trees and shrubs planted in the very late twenties, the foothills gardener is plagued by late and early frosts. But the soil is fertile and drought less likely to be severe than on the open prairie, and this made gardening easier even in the early days when extra water had to be pumped from a well and carried to the plants. At Cottonwoods the water was hard and cold when it came from the wells. Specially favoured plants were treated to rain water, conserved in barrels fed from the roof by eavestroughs but that was an erratic supply, though it would be eked out by tubs of well water allowed to warm in the summer sun and sometimes enriched by the ample supply of manure the stock provided.

Though frost restricted the variety of plants, shrubs and trees, the fertility of the soil and the long hours of summer sunlight produced rapid growth when enough moisture was available. There was some experiment with native plants and especially with trees; Cottonwoods has several spruce transplanted from nearer Sheep Creek seventy years or more past. The aspen poplar did well as a specimen tree but for shelter the green ash and the Russian poplar, distributed from government nurseries, were easier to grow in the requisite numbers. The range of ornamental plants that could be grown expanded rapidly, often by experiment with seed from the increasing number of suppliers, and by the exchange of seed and plants with other gardeners.

Among the hardy perennials that did exceedingly well was the delphinium, introduced at Cottonwoods about 1930 and still a striking feature of my sister's borders, though the hops and the white daisy that dominated earlier photographs are no longer so much in evidence. Maltese Cross or Scarlet Lychnis was another old fashioned cottage garden perennial that did well in Sheep Creek gardens and was perhaps one of the earliest introduced. The Iceland poppy was a general favourite which flourished under the semi-alpine conditions as did a number of other poppies. The quiet persistence of many of the violas was early appreciated and pansies, given enough moisture and a minimum of protection, could produce blossoms of impressive size. The late and early frosts did restrict the early gardener to the hardier flowers, annual as well as perennial, but as time passed the range of possibility expanded, as the gardens of Millarville today, and the annual flower festival at Christ Church, so amply demonstrate.

It was in the foothills of southern Alberta that I acquired a taste for gardening. For the last thirty years, however, it is in the rather different conditions of central Alberta, on a lakeside about forty miles west of Edmonton, that I have been able to indulge that taste and with the assistance of my family and friends, develop a garden that has become a central preoccupation in my years of retirement.

Lakeside gardening has for me a special interest because I am convinced that a lakeside garden has its own climate and a highly idiosyncratic climate at that. I have not kept proper records but I am convinced that some parts of the garden have a substantially longer growing season than others. Even a few yards make a difference and other factors are obviously the distance above the lake level and the amount of shelter available, both highly variable even in this small area. For weeks in April and early May, and from late August into October, the nights tremble on the verge of frost, but often we escape. We cover some of the tender plants, tomatoes for example, but I am more and more inclined to depend upon the benign influence of the lake. In 1986 we used leaf lettuce until well into October

In the garden of Robert and Carole Plante in Coleman.

and the Russell lupins, which admittedly had had an exceptionally good year, were still producing respectable blooms until we had a really hard frost in the last week of that month.

As our garden at Kapasiwin lies at the east end of Lake Wabamun, it is exposed to the prevailing winds from the west. This makes it difficult to maintain snow cover on westward facing banks but the wind also brings in sand to our beaches and all the flotsam and jetsam of a lake sixteen miles long passing into what the ecologists call eutrophication. One of the by-products of this process is a plentiful supply of lake weed. What Kapasiwin has for a long time called "the weed problem" is a fact of life on Lake Wabamun that has many aspects. One of the more agreeable of these is that the harvested weed provides a useful winter mulch. By the spring it has virtually disappeared, leaving a residue that is as much sand as humus. Whether this has any value as plant food is a matter for argument but I am convinced that it is an efficient soil conditioner.

The lake not only provides our special climate but it is also the dominant feature of our view, for we can look westward along its length for fifteen miles or more. The lake is to our Kapasiwin garden what the view up Sheep Creek towards the Rockies is to the garden at Cottonwoods. The prairie landscape has often been portrayed as intimidating the settler, but perhaps because of the gentle contours and modest scale of Sheep Creek's valley, the early arrivals there seem to have responded with enthusiasm to the majestic prospects of the mountains and sited their houses to take advantage of them. This sensitivity to the positive values of landscape is reflected in the names they chose, "Hillside", "Viewfield", "Springhill", "Riverside", "Cottonwoods". The desire to enjoy the many moods of the lakeside landscape from as many points of vantage as possible dictates the design of a garden as much as the pressure to provide an environment that plants will find congenial.

Since we settled at Kapasiwin more than thirty years ago three major power plants have been built, two at the lake's edge and in full sight, the third mercifully screened by the almost untouched wooded shore of an Indian reserve. On the western horizon can be seen the results of the open cast coal mining which feeds the thermal plants from the coal deposits which lie around and, alas, below the lake. Behind our cottage lies the main line of the Canadian National, now double-tracked. The railway made Lake Wabamun accessible to summer cottagers when it was built more than seventy years ago; even thirty years ago transcontinental trains could still be stopped on request at the rustic station the railway considered appropriate to a summer village. The power plants are more recent intrusions but, although they are said to have a prescribed life, few of us expect to see them crumble into picturesque ruin. Perhaps some ingenious geneticist will develop a winter-hardy ivy. Meanwhile they, like the railway, serve by their ruthless functionalism to define the view from our gardens.

If a garden gives pleasure by providing vantage points from which to enjoy a prospect, that pleasure is enhanced if the garden gives a sense of privacy, of enclosure, of protection, of seclusion. In a sense prospect and privacy are contradictory but one can plan a garden to effect a reconciliation. Our Kapasiwin garden is a narrow strip along the lake shore on the west, more or less, and the access road, paralleling the railway on the east. The road is technically a private one and is certainly a dead-end. It has long been so designated by appropriate signs but these have never seemed convincing to the motoring public. When we and our neighbours began to build our cottages we provided hours of innocent amusement to explorers of Lake Wabamun's environs, who would park their cars, eat their sandwiches and enjoy our antics, occasionally rewarding us with an empty cigarette package, an orange peel or the wrapping from a chocolate bar.

Our lot was too narrow to build the forest wall that protected the pioneer gardens of New England and the Canadas, and was reproduced by the shelter belts of the prairies. I borrowed from the ranching tradition, found a small local sawmill, no longer, unfortunately, in being, and built a slab fence, like the ones that had given shelter to the corrals of my childhood. The slabs, the unwanted sides sawn off spruce poles, were put up with their bark still on. Here again I borrowed from my Millarville experience. Christ Church was built from unpeeled logs; when, after more than thirty years, the bark was stripped so that preservatives could be applied, obliging worms, though long deceased, had decorated the logs with an intricate and charming tracery. Our slabs are now free of bark, agreeably patterned and weathered to a pleasing grey that gives an excellent background to the perennial border that the fence shelters.

The use of local materials gives a profound satisfaction and helps, I am sure, to harmonize the garden with its setting. Our garden has two levels, the upper level along the road, with our main cottage and our kitchen garden, and the lower level along the lake. The two levels are separated by what must once

Bougainvillaea along the side of the house of Arthur and Theresa Patterson, Priddis. One of a number of plants they start in their greenhouse and transplant to their summer garden.

Iris, Devonian Gardens, near Devon.

have been the bank of the lake. This bank was well treed with saskatoon, pincherry, red willow, aspen poplar and, at the south end, black poplar. The latter were mature enough to be dangerous and they have been taken out, leaving enough saskatoons to produce an annual crop of the best of our native small fruit. An old path at about the middle of the bank was made safer by the use as steps of old railway ties, of which the double-tracking program of our neighbour produced a generous supply at a modest price. Putting the ties in place disclosed that only a thin layer of soil covered sizeable boulders and these, supplemented by others like them, formed the rudiments of a rock garden. It certainly does not measure up to the purist's specifications but rock plants seem to like it.

To supplement the trees and shrubs already on the bank we have planted a number of spruce, Scotch pine and mountain ash, and near the cottage we have allowed the native chokecherry to multiply, to the qualified delight of a series of migrant birds. Originally we had thought we might grade the bank but it proved difficult to mow. What was something of a problem area became an asset when a forester friend introduced me to the two junipers native to our foothills region to the west. These have done extremely well and now I am trying to propagate them, as I have not been able to find them in nurseries. Many other junipers flourish under our lakeside conditions but none better than these two native Albertans,

which provide a magnificent ground cover and are more urbane in their habits than some of their sophisticated cousins.

There is no end to the adventure of even the smallest lakeside garden or to the joy of discovering that it can provide a congenial home for plants that have a reputation for an unwillingness to settle permanently in the prairie west. Primulas, for example, once dismissed as only the foible of the nostalgic Englishmen, are the mainstay of our spring garden and survive our hardest winter, though they are grateful for water in a dry season. Daffodils prefer the lower land, close to the lake, where they can root themselves in moist sand and still enjoy the cool brisk wind off the lake. They, like the other bulbs, go quickly if, as occasionally happens, scorching heat comes in May or early June. The heat brings on the nemesias, the colourful annual which I first saw about 1929, planted at the old Bretton Hall Hotel in Banff. My mother fell in love with it then and planted it annually at Cottonwoods. At Kapasiwin we use it to overplant the daffodils to conceal their drying foliage. It bridges the gap between the daffodils and the hollyhocks which, rather to my surprise, have flourished in the same bed and seed themselves year after year. The seed originally came from an old garden in Garneau, near the university on Edmonton's south side. The plants that mingle comfortably in a single corner reflect, and certainly do not exhaust, the wealth of Alberta's gardening tradition.

August wedding at Christ Church, Millarville. The flowers are part of the annual Millarville flower show, held earlier in the day.

Monkshood in the garden at "Cottonwoods."

# Excerpts from
## *ANNORA BROWN*
## *SKETCHES FROM LIFE*

I was brought up in two worlds.

There was the real world of great prairie distances, high skies, foothills, blue mountains, berry picking, snow, wind, frostbite, mosquitoes, humble frame houses, elevators, wheat fields. That was my home. I grew up there.

There was also a dream world where nothing ever went amiss. A world of castles, beautiful churches with marvellous choirs, concert halls, trees, sugaring off parties in the maple woods, ocean waves, sandy beaches. That was the world of the grown-ups. All the adults that I knew had been born in wonderful places called Down East, the Old Country, Home.

It seemed that someone was always feeling sorry for me. "What a pity that she has to grow up in a place like this."

In early spring I watched eagerly for the first flower. Finding a small yellow cinquefoil blooming close to the earth, I would exclaim, "Look! Look! I found a buttercup!"

"That is not a buttercup," I would be told. "I wish you could see the buttercups that grew in our meadow at home. As high as your waist and shiny yellow."

"Well, what is this then?"

"I don't know, but it is not a buttercup."

The dainty hood's phlox that formed mats of white blossoms against mosslike foliage, I called mayflower because it bloomed in May. But it was not mayflower. That grew in the woods of Nova Scotia and was sweet smelling.

Robins were not robins. English robins were small, colourful, and perky. The purple vetch that made carpets of colour over the hillsides in June compared unfavourably with the heather on the hills of Scotland. The river bottom, looking like a bride in a shimmering veil of saskatoon and choke cherry blossoms, was not a orchard. Bluebells were not bluebells. "I just wish you could see the lakes of bluebells in the woods at home." A crocus was not a crocus. Geese were not swans. Gophers were not squirrels.

Too bad! Too bad! Too bad!

I was passionately loyal to my own country. Kicking at a stone in frustration at living in such a negative world, I asked, "Is the Old Country really a lot nicer than here?"

My father said, "Stop kicking that stone. You will wear out your shoes." He was interested in practical matters.

My mother, so alert to the struggles of my mind, so wise in guiding it to larger thinking, said emphatically, "No. Those people are thinking of their childhoods. They can't see what is in front of them for looking at what is behind them. Don't

Mary Dover, in her country garden outside Calgary. She is the granddaughter of Colonel J. F. Macleod, who established the Northwest Mounted Police in Alberta and after whom Fort Macleod is named.

spoil your life by looking in far corners for what is right before your eyes."

... When I think of my home now, I think first of the garden. My earliest memory is of a gravel- and rock-strewn area stretching to the far horizon. Then came a fence that closed it in, rocks and all. My parents, with my mother as the moving spirit, slowly built bed after bed for flowering plants and a large

Backyard, Coleman. The coal mining communities of the Crowsnest Pass are known for their small but beautifully tended gardens.

vegetable garden from which we gathered fresh vegetables for the summer, and a winter's supply of potatoes, onions, carrots, peas, turnips, beets. Nothing tasted better than the parsnips, left in the ground over winter and dug up as soon as the ground thawed. This first taste of spring shared honours with the early flowers, the returning robins, and meadow larks. In time all the common, hardy plants burst into a riot of colour. Tucked in amongst them were others that had been labelled in eastern catalogues, which were all my mother had, "not hardy on the prairies". At the back of the garden was planted a tiny crab-apple sapling which took root and flourished.

When my mother could no longer work in her garden, my father and I struggled to keep it in its original condition, at first for her pleasure and finally in her memory.

It is difficult for two people of varying temperaments to share a garden. As time went by we had our problems. My father was a "hoer". With his background of military training he liked things in straight, easily cultivated rows. I was a "planter". I liked things to grow as they would in Nature. Often for my paintings of wild flowers I would dig an entire plant with all its surrounding soil and grass. I would do a painting of it and then plant it in the garden. My father would hoe it out. At last we came to an agreement that certain parts were his: other areas were mine. Margaret, with her enthusiasm for using native plants, would bring great bundles of things she had found in the wilds. She would plant them for me helter-skelter, without

regard to rights. After she had gone they would be carefully removed and planted beyond the reach of my father's hoe. My father's garden kept us in vegetables, tomatoes, and roses. My part of the garden flourished too. Though my farmer-neighbour, with tongue-in-cheek, threatened to report me to the weed inspector, people who were interested in my efforts came from a hundred miles away to see my garden. I could delight my colour sense with Gaillardia, prickly pear, and prairie mallow blending in exciting colour harmony. I could marvel at hepaticas from Ontario blooming side by side with prairie anemone, or at jack-in-the-pulpits from the East sharing a bed with calypso from the mountains.

Then came the gradual realization that my father was no longer able to cope with so much and that I was too busy to do my share. Flower bed after flower bed was turned into lawn. But the garden was still a haven, an outdoor living room where we spent much of our day and entertained our friends. Under the shade of the apple tree, we sat talking in groups that ranged in age from crawlers to my father who was nearing ninety.

. . . As I worked in the upstairs room which I dignified by the name of "studio", life went on around me in the garden. The growth of trees and shrubs throughout the town attracted countless birds. In winter English sparrows were joined by flocks of Bohemian waxwings that greedily gobbled every last berry from the mountain ash; by flocks of evening grosbeaks that ripped the seeds from the maples and covered the snow with husks; and by the odd scarlet pine grosbeak that took shelter in the vines. From my window I also saw redpolls, woodpeckers, chickadees, snowbirds.

In spring and in autumn my bird books were in constant use as I strove to identify the many migrating species.

In summer the busy house wren kept up an excited paean of joy to the world. A goldfinch nested in the lilacs. Kingbirds chattered about their nest in the maples while an oriole fluted its "pity-oo, pity-oo" from a high branch. The patter of the sprinkler and the smell of water on wet grass floated up to me.

Looking out, I would see my father leaning on his hoe, waiting patiently for his pet robin to pick up the worms he had unearthed. Or perhaps he would be sitting under the white-blossomed, pink-budded apple tree as he whistled softly to a mountain blue bird that was building its nest in a box over his head.

Houses and gardens in the Gold Bar district of Edmonton.

Prize sweet peas, Millarville Flower Show.

A neighbour's greeting, seven in the morning on a Sunday, Coleman.

# Excerpt from
## *NIBBLES AND FEASTS*
by
Judy Schultz
"Cornpatch politics"

Each year in August, when the corn is high and the sun is hot, I go home to Saskatchewan. The great pleasure of the place is an intense concern with the quality of life.

It's 11:30 of a hot August morning. On the back burner of the kitchen stove, a big aluminum roaster half full of water is going blip-blip-bubble as it comes to a boil. Outside in the cornpatch, two of us stand shoulder-deep in Golden Bantam.

"It's short this year," notes my mother-in-law, the keeper of the patch. "Hasn't been enough rain to float a toothpick."

It's quiet here. The only sound comes from a diesel horn out on the highway. Together we move down the rows, picking fat green ears with toast-brown tassels while my dog, Tuffy, chases imaginary gophers. I love the satisfying snap each time I break off an ear, and the squeaking sound as I rip husk from cob. Most of all I love the smell, like fresh-cut grass.

"We used to do these in a washboiler when we had five hired men," she says. With a couple of dozen cobs in her basket, she's heading for the kitchen when an aunt rounds the corner with an armful of cucumbers.

*Aunt:* Elma, you're *not* putting that corn to boil now. It's twenty minutes until dinner.

*Mother:* That's right. It takes twenty minutes to cook corn.

*Aunt:* Never! Five minutes is all! In twenty minutes you'll cook all the good out of it!

*Mother:* I've been cooking it twenty minutes all my life and it's always tasted pretty good to me!

*(Exit mother to kitchen, carrying corn and looking determined. Aunt-with-cucumbers trots behind, dispensing advice and predicting disaster in the corn pot. Tuffy and I bring up the rear.)*

The day is saved by the arrival of a second aunt who had invited us to a coffee party that afternoon. She looks worn out.

"She's probably been up all night polishing spoons," says the cucumber aunt, who has a way with words.

Wrong. She's been driving a grain truck. Harvest has begun and the coffee party is off, because this tiny woman who'll never see seventy again is as much at home behind the wheel of a truck as she is behind the handle of a coffee pot.

There's a short discussion of bushels per acre (hectares are not a part of their vocabulary, and they'll fight anyone who tries to change it). Somebody mentions that Cliff Johnson's two-and-a-half-pound tomato made the front page of the local paper. But the corn issue is about to rise again, and the cucumber aunt addresses the grain hauler.

"How long do *you* usually cook corn?"

Four women and a dog are suddenly silent. The only sound is the blip-blip-blop from the corn pot.

"As long as it takes," she snaps, and whizzes out the door.

Annora Brown, *Prairie Anemone, ca.* 1953, linocut.

# NEXT YEAR COUNTRY

Janet Mitchell, *A Queer Sort of Day*, 1974, watercolour.

Watering horses along the shore of Hand Hills Lake. This region of the province was among the hardest hit by drought and depression in the 1930s.

# IT'S GOTTA RAIN
# SOMETIME

by
R. Ross Annett

In the seventh year of the drought, the tractor that had been buried in the soil-blowing of 1932 came unexpectedly to light.

Babe and Little Joe found it. They came bursting into the kitchen, their eyes snapping with excitement. Their bare hands were blue with cold, for it was a raw March day and they had no mittens. They had no stockings either. Bare legs and feet showed here and there through rents in overalls and shoes.

In the five years of her life, Babe had never had anything but boy's clothing — "and damn little of that," as her father put it.

"Pop!" cried eight-year-old Little Joe shrilly. "There's a pipe — a kind of a rusty stovepipe — stickin' outta the side o' that sand pile!"

"On Uncle Pete's place," explained Babe. "A wusty pipe."

"I scraped the sand away," Little Joe continued breathlessly, "an' it goes down an' down — the pipe does."

"It's a gopher's chimney, I bet."

"G'wan! Gophers don't have chimneys."

"Or a bogeyman's," suggested Babe.

"Or a tractor's, Baby," said Big Joe. "A tractor's exhaust pipe."

"Whose tractor, Pop?"

Big Joe finished peeling the spuds for dinner and set them on the stove. He emptied the peelings into an old pail for Uncle Pete. He would not let Uncle Pete peel the potatoes, because Uncle Pete made the peelings so thick. He used them in his still.

"Whose tractor, Pop?" Babe persisted.

"Ourn, Baby," said Big Joe, glancing across at Uncle Pete, who sat beside the window, tinkering with a length of copper pipe that had once been the feed pipe of a car.

The swell car Big Joe had bought in 1930. The year he and Emmy and Little Joe had spent the winter in California.

The car still sat where the garage had been, a forlorn reminder of happier days.

Bit by bit, at times when fuel was scarce, Big Joe had dismantled the garage. Uncle Pete had removed from the car any parts that were useful for his still. It was just a wreck now, and the kids used it to play in.

"I never knew we had a tractor," said Babe.

"We've had six tractors, Baby. Bought two in '26," Big Joe reminisced pleasantly, "an' another in '27. Paid cash for 'em, too. That's the way we did them days. In the spring of '32 we traded 'em in on three new ones. We never made no payments on them. The machine company took two of 'em away, but they couldn't find the third one."

"You buried it," piped Little Joe, chuckling at Pop's cleverness.

"Nope," Big Joe said. "Wind buried it. An' now the wind's uncovering it again, I guess."

"The Lord taketh away an' the Lord giveth," wheezed Uncle Pete facetiously. A faint gleam showed in his bleary eyes. He was recalling the fact that beside the tractor, and buried with it, was a granary with perhaps a hundred bushels of wheat in it.

Big Joe remembered the day the machine-company men came after the tractors that he could not pay for. That was in 1933.

"Where's the other tractor?" they had demanded.

"Buried," said Big Joe.

"Buried!" cried the machine agent. "What the hell for?"

"For eternity, brother," said Big Joe. " 'Nless you bring a steam shovel to dig her out."

The men had gone with him across the road to Uncle Pete's half section. He showed them the big sand dune that had accumulated in one of the worst blows — and had grown since — completely burying tractor and granary.

The men had gone away then, and they never came back. They never expected to see that tractor again.

But if the exhaust stack of the tractor was showing, the dune must be moving on. It would not take much digging to uncover both tractor and granary. And, Big Joe ruminated, the granary contained enough wheat to seed a partial crop — a hundred acres or so. He could use the tractor to sow it — if he could get some tractor fuel and some oil.

The trouble was that nobody would advance him seed or fuel anymore. Everybody thought that the country would never come back, that it ought to be abandoned. Most people, indeed, had moved out.

But not Big Joe. He would not abandon the section of land that had brought him more than one ten-thousand-dollar crop of wheat since he left his North Dakota birthplace to settle in Canada. True, during the past six years his farm had often not produced feed enough for one cow and a scrawny team of horses, let alone a crop. But Big Joe stuck.

"It's gotta rain sometime," he kept saying.

They had had no milk since they ate the cow to keep her from starving to death; no eggs since they ate the hens for the same reason.

Uncle Pete stayed on, too. He used to grumble a lot about a man having nothing to live for if he could not buy liquor. But he kept on living. Never amiable or talkative at any time, during the first few years of the drought he grew more and more morose.

Then one autumn when they got their relief potatoes, Uncle Pete conceived the idea of making a still, and life had taken on a new interest for him. From their potato peelings and those he collected from the few remaining neighbours, Uncle Pete distilled a satisfying liquor. He worked steadily, for he had nothing else to do and he had a pessimistic feeling that the drought would last for years. Big Joe was sure Uncle Pete had a lot of liquor cached away.

Very occasionally, when he needed money, he sold a little. He never gave any away. He would not give you a drink, Uncle Pete wouldn't, not to save your soul.

He might just as well have been a hermit, so utterly solitary was his life. Nobody bothered about him or talked to him much. He seemed less human than the mongrel dog that slunk hungrily about the place — just an old soak, with his mottled, shapeless face and his clothes that had been nondescript in their best days and were now mere rags.

Only Babe, who was too young to know better rated him as humanly individual, and therefore interesting.

Big Joe did not drink. He had promised Emmy.

"Don't get to be an old soak like Uncle Pete," Emmy used to say, "for the kids' sake."

But sometimes in these last years Big Joe caught himself envying Uncle Pete. Life had grown so sour. Whereas, in bad years as in good, Uncle Pete still had his liquor.

Emmy had been lucky, too. She had died before drought and poverty took all the fun out of life. If a fellow could die young — or else a fellow might get a little fun if he could see his kids having some fun.

Dinner would have been a quiet meal but for the excited chatter of Babe and Little Joe. Big Joe's mind was on that tractor and the seed wheat. He ate his dry potatoes without really tasting them. They had potatoes for dinner and oatmeal porridge for breakfast and supper.

If he could get fuel and oil for the tractor and get that wheat sown, why maybe it might rain this year. It just naturally had to rain sometime.

Apparently Uncle Pete was thinking of the wheat, too. Big Joe had to remind him about eating with his knife.

"How the hell can we make Baby a lady if you don't set her an example?" Big Joe demanded, pointing accusingly with his own knife at the culprit.

Uncle Pete accepted the reprimand meekly. He appeared to realize that Babe had to be brought up right. Sometimes his bleary eyes rested upon Babe with a faint awareness, as though he were thinking: "In an otherwise drab world, ain't she somethin'!"

After dinner they all went over to Uncle Pete's place to see the tractor. And there she was — or, at least, there her exhaust stack was — sticking out of the sand as perky as a gopher's snout on the first warm day of spring.

"Another good blow of wind from the right direction, or a few hours' work with a shovel, and she'll be in the clear," Big Joe figured. The granary, still invisible under the slope of the dune, would not be hard to reach either.

Uncle Pete's eyes showed a dull wistfulness, and Big Joe knew he was thinking of one hundred bushels of wheat in terms of the store liquor it would buy. But Big Joe was thinking of the crop of wheat it would make if seeded, and if it rained. Food and clothing and school and fun for Babe and Little Joe.

"Now," he planned busily, "we got some seed and we got a tractor. If somebody will stake us to fuel and oil — " He was interrupted by a snort of disgust from Uncle Pete, and whirled angrily. "You want that Baby should go on growin' up like she is? Well, she ain't gonna — not if I can help it."

Work boots on the farm of Harlan Greene, Dewberry.

*Opposite:*
Evening, Pincher.

Inez French and her nephew Curtis, baling straw, west of Hill Spring.

He fancied he could read a shamefaced look on Uncle Pete's almost unreadable face, and he continued more kindly:

"You keep on drinkin' your old spud licker for a while. If we get a crop, Little Joe and Babe and me'll go places. An' you can buy plenty of store licker. What d'ya say, kids?"

"Damn tootin'!" said Little Joe.

"Damn tootin'!" echoed Babe.

"Ladies don't say 'damn,' Baby."

"Why don't they, Pop?"

"Well, just because they're ladies, see?"

"I don' wanna be a lady. Whadda I wanna be a lady for?"

"Why, dammit, because I promised your mom, Baby."

Little Joe was curious. "What'll she do when she's a lady, Pop?"

"Oh, ride around in cars and look pretty."

"Gee!" gasped Little Joe. "Will we have a car?"

"Damn tootin'!" Big Joe promised. "If we get a crop."

And Uncle Pete wheezed pessimistically: "If we get some tractor fuel. An' if it rains."

The next day Big Joe drove to town in his rickety old democrat, whereof the front wheels toed in and the back ones wobbled astonishingly. The tires were held on with hay wire and rattled noisily. His horses were a pathetically bony team of grays that had wintered on Russian thistle, and looked it.

"Couldn't rightly call them specimens of horseflesh," Big Joe said. "Bones an' hide is all they got."

Big Joe took the kids with him because even a trip to Benson was an event for them — Benson, which had only been a hamlet in the good times and was now nothing but a huddle of weathered shacks, most of them deserted. But the kids had never been places and seen things like Big Joe and Emmy — at least, Babe had not been places, and Little Joe had been too young to notice.

On the road, Big Joe entertained them with stories of the "good times." It was his favourite topic and the kids loved it. He told them how he and Emmy used to get in the car and roll in to Benson — or farther still, to Sanford — and load up with things to wear and things to eat. Oranges, boxes of apples — all they wanted to eat in those days. Babe, of course, did not know about apples and oranges, and Little Joe had only seen them in Hindson's store. But Big Joe made their eyes glisten as he told them about them.

Having prodded the horses up a long rise, they caught sight of Benson. Big Joe told them of the six huge grain elevators that had once been required to handle the big wheat crops of the district. Only one remained now, and that was closed. Benson was sure dead. It made Big Joe feel bad to see the "So-this-is-Paris" look in the kids' eyes as their democrat clattered down the one gravelly street — to think that they had seen so little that a dump like Benson gave them a thrill!

Ed Hindson's was the only store left. Ed had fallen heir to many jobs as people moved out. He was storekeeper, postmaster, undertaker, sold gas and oil, if any; handled express and freight for the one train per week that the railroad ran over the branch. In fact, Ed did all the business that was done in Benson. And he had plenty of spare time. Ed was too old to move when the drought came. He said he was going to stay on in Benson until he just naturally dried up and blew away like the Russian thistle.

In court, an accused person is considered innocent until proved guilty. In Hindson's store a person is considered broke until he proves otherwise. You had to tell Ed what you wanted and show him the money to pay for it before he would get up out of his chair by the pot-bellied stove. That's what six years of drought had done to Ed Hindson. He was glad to see you, though; there were so few people to talk to.

Big Joe approached the matter of tractor fuel nervously. He hated to ask for favours, he who had always paid cash when he had cash. Also, he did not want to let on about the tractor, at least until he got his crop seeded. The machine agent had moved out, leaving Ed as the company's representative, but the company would seize the tractor fast enough if they heard about it.

"Look, Ed," he began. "I can get seed wheat and I can get the use of a tractor to do the seedin'. All I need is fuel and oil for the tractor, and if — I wondered if you'd stake me to that. If I get a crop — "

He began to flounder because he saw that Ed was not registering enthusiasm. Ed was drawing hard on a battered pipe, and the smell of the tobacco made Big Joe faint as with hunger. He had not had any tobacco himself since God-knows-when.

Ed was rubbing his bald head with one hand and squinting through the tobacco smoke at Babe, where she stood beside the stove, dimpling shyly and hanging on to Big Joe's ragged pantleg. Looking down at her, Big Joe realized all at once that she had a poor colour — pasty, almost. Little Joe was the same. Oatmeal and potatoes did not make a balanced diet for growing kids.

Ed Hindson spat on the stove and it sizzled. His slitted eyes glinted angrily.

"Lookit, Joe," he said at last. "You take them kids outta this country and I'll help you all I can to get away. But, to put in another crop — My God, you're dumb, Joe! Won't you ever realize it's quit rainin'? It ain't ever goin' to rain no more here."

"It's gotta rain sometime," Big Joe insisted.

"Why's it gotta?"

Eventually, Big Joe abandoned the hopeless argument. But he was bitterly disappointed. It was sure going to be tough if a few dollars' worth of gas and oil was going to stand between him and a crop.

After a while he remembered an errand he had promised to do for Uncle Pete.

"Listen, Ed, could you spare Uncle Pete an empty five-gallon oil can for his — he wants a five-gallon can. He told me to ask you."

"I guess maybe," said Ed. "There's one right behind you — not that one — the one next to it."

Big Joe picked up the can and set it down again. He had a sudden desperate idea. He would talk a while and then absent-mindedly pick up the wrong can and walk out with five gallons of tractor oil. That would be a start toward his seeding requirements and Ed might not notice what was happening.

So he sat on the counter and listened to Ed talk about Japan and China. Big Joe could not afford a newspaper, so that, as far as news of the outside world was concerned, he was like a man down a well. He never heard what was going on outside unless someone like Ed Hindson came to the edge and called down to him.

"Well, kids," he said at last, "guess we better be hittin' the trail."

He picked up a full can of oil trying to handle it as though it were empty.

Babe piped shrilly, "You got the wrong can, Pop!"

Big Joe could almost have slapped her.

"Why, dammit, so I have!" he ejaculated.

He exchanged the cans with the elaborately innocent manner of a man caught stealing five gallons of oil. "Well, so long, Ed," he growled.

"Wait."

Ed Hindson hobbled behind the counter and filled a large bag with oranges, which he presented to Babe and Little Joe.

"It's criminal," he muttered to himself, and he was referring to the obvious effects of malnutrition in the kids' faces, not to Big Joe's attempted theft. That was kind of pathetic.

"First time he ever tried to pinch anything in his life," Ed thought. "An' after six years of drought he'd steal, if necessary, to get another crop in. Some people never learn."

He watched them cross the street to the democrat — the gaunt and shabby farmer and the ragged boy and girl. He saw the kids dig into the bag of oranges, saw Big Joe refuse an orange and walk down the street. Big Joe had a fondness for oranges, too, Ed remembered. He himself had often seen Big Joe eat three and four at a time when he could afford to buy them.

Suddenly Ed ambled around the counter, picked up two cans of oil and carried them across the street. He put them in the back of the democrat.

"Tell your pop he can have this much oil, but it's all I can afford. He'll have to get gas someplace else."

"Just encouragin' him in foolishness, but what the hell!" he growled as he returned to the store.

A big man in a big new car drove in to Big Joe's place a week later. Big Joe guessed that he was a government man. Guessed likely Ed Hindson sent him. Only government men could afford cars nowadays. If it were not for government men, Joe guessed the automobile factories would have to close down. And if everybody got jobs with the government, who the aitch would raise wheat?

This man was an "orderin' " kind of fellow, too, and Big Joe never "ordered" worth a cent. The stranger began by practically ordering Big Joe to let himself and family be moved to someplace where they could raise feed for a cow at least.

"You owe it to your kids," he declared. But he brought that point up late in the argument, after Joe's mind was set.

Uncle Pete and the kids were admiring the car.

"I know them kind of places you'd move me to," said Big Joe. "Places where you can raise enough vegetables an' such to just live on. One crop of wheat and I'll make more money than them folks do in a lifetime. How come you got money to move me an' the family, but you won't advance me forty-fifty dollars for gas to put a crop in?"

"I'm not allowed to," said the stranger, "because you can't get a crop of wheat in this country. It's got to be abandoned."

"Come around at the end of July and maybe I'll talk to you," was all Big Joe would concede, and the man climbed into his shiny car and drove away.

Country Fair, Lac La Biche.

Summer road.

Evening mist west of Plamondon, a French-Canadian farming district in northern Alberta.

Fresh produce at Cranford in the Taber corn belt.

"Likely he'll stop at Benson — he better had," wheezed Uncle Pete at Big Joe's elbow.

"What do you care where he stops?"

Uncle Pete made asthmatic noises that might have been a chuckle.

"If he don't stop at Benson, he'll find himself outta gas, that's all," he said. "I siphoned 'bout eight gallons outta his gas tank."

Big Joe stared, open-mouthed, at Uncle Pete. Sometimes he wondered if the purple-veined mask that was Uncle Pete's face could ever have been smooth and clear like Babe's. But he was not thinking about that now.

"It's an idea," he muttered. "If we only had enough people come here in cars —"

It was time to get on the land and Big Joe was growing anxious. He and Uncle Pete had dug the tractor out and tinkered it into shape. And they had shovelled a way into the granary. But he had been to Sanford and canvassed everyone he knew, in a vain effort to get gasoline on credit. He had nothing on the place which was worth selling; not even the team of feeble old horses would bring any money.

With the oil Ed Hindson had provided and the gas Uncle Pete had pilfered, they got the tractor running. They hooked the tractor to a disk with the seed-drill behind that. They had to disk and seed in one operation, for they could not afford to go over the land twice. Anyway, it was light soil, and windblown, so it worked easy.

"You go ahead — as far as eight gallons'll take you," Big Joe told Uncle Pete. "I'll be back tonight with some gas."

He put an old gasoline drum in the back of the democrat, hitched up the team and drove ten miles to Sanford. There were no cars in Benson. This time he did not take the kids. He did not want them to witness what he was about to do. And, besides, he might be arrested.

The meadowlarks were whistling cheerfully as he drove along. Big Joe liked meadowlarks. He admired them because they could sure take it — whistling cheerful defiance to cold or drought.

Big Joe could take it, too. There was enough of the boy in him to thrill to the challenge of wintry winds, to delight in bird songs. The sweep of dawn across the prairie, the far-flung sunsets, moved him as glorious sound symphonies might move

some men. And those were things that even poverty could not deprive him of.

But those things did not buy grub for Babe and Little Joe or put colour in their cheeks. They needed more than potatoes and oatmeal, even if he could stand it. So Big Joe was embarked on a career of crime.

He regretted it, though. He knew that he would not get the same pleasure from the meadowlarks' songs anymore.

Court was sitting in Sanford and there were many cars parked all around the courthouse block. Big Joe found an empty space and pulled his team to the curb between two parked cars.

He had two empty pails hanging from the reach of the democrat, in each pail a sufficient length of rubber tubing. He unscrewed the cap on the gas tank of the nearest car, pushed one end of each tube in and then sucked on the other ends until he got a mouthful of gasoline. Then he dropped one of the free ends in each pail and stood by while the stuff siphoned, examining the hub of the democrat wheel with such obvious innocence that anyone observing him would have become suspicious at once.

Also, he wrote down the car's license number. When he got a crop he was going to give back to the car owner two pails of gasoline.

When the pails were nearly full, he replaced the cap on the gas tank, backed his team out carefully, so as not to set the pails swinging, and drove to a deserted alley. There, unobserved, he poured the contents of the pails into the drum on the democrat. Then he reslung the pails to the reach and cruised around the block, looking for a new parking place.

It was tedious work. More, it was tense and nerve-wracking. Big Joe had never stolen a nickel in his life, and sometimes, when people passed on the sidewalk, the perspiration oozed from him, he was sure, faster than the gasoline flowed into the pails beneath the democrat.

Once two men came out of the side door of the courthouse and approached the car next to the one Big Joe had been working on — just as he was backing out from the curb.

"I smell gas," he heard one of the men say. "I wonder is that feedline leaking again."

As Joe drove away, he noticed the fellow with his head under the hood of the car.

He had been late getting to town, and court was over before he had filled the drum. But he got a few more bucketfuls from cars parked in front of restaurants.

As he drove out of town in the dusk of the spring evening, he noticed cars parked along the street where the movie theatre was. There was still a movie in Sanford. North of town, the drought had not hit so hard. People always got a partial crop there. But the farther you went south, the worse it got. Joe lived ten miles south.

The sight of the cars by the theatre gave Joe an idea. If he kept mooching around in daylight, somebody was bound to get suspicious. But after dark it ought to be safer.

It was after midnight when he got home, but he was up with the first hint of dawn. When there was work to do, Big Joe never felt fatigue.

"I'll run the tractor this morning," he told Uncle Pete. "This afternoon you can spell me off while I go to town for more gas."

Uncle Pete asked no questions. He did not need to.

Big Joe rode the roaring tractor all morning, round and round Uncle Pete's hundred-acre field. He wished they had enough seed for the rest of Uncle Pete's half section and his own six hundred and forty acres. But with one hundred acres of crop, he would be back in the money again anyway.

The tractor thundered along in a cloud of dust, dragging the disk and the seed-drill behind it. In the very centre of the dust cloud Big Joe sat at the wheel of the tractor, dreaming dreams of food, and clothing and fun for Babe and Little Joe — picturing them with the colour of health in their faces while his own face grew black with dirt until he looked like a blackface comedian in a minstrel show.

In the afternoon, Uncle Pete relieved him, so that he could drive in town with another empty drum on the democrat. And the early darkness found him plying his new trade up and down the street where the movie theatre was.

It was easier in the dark. Sometimes he did not even bother to drive away, but emptied the pails into the drum right there on the street. Nobody paid any attention to a nondescript farmer messing about a democrat. His nervousness of the day before decreased until at times he was able to meditate dreamily while the pails filled. How he would bring the kids in to the show sometimes. They had never seen a movie. He pictured them, round-eyed with the wonder of it. There was a lot of fun in the world for kids.

It was late when he pulled in to what he thought would be his final call of the evening. He thought the drum was nearly full. No doubt he had grown careless. He had unscrewed the cap on the gas tank of a car and had just got the siphon tubes

Ball diamond, Nebraska Community Hall. The Nebraska Niners host East Bend, a community on the shore of nearby Buffalo Lake. The predecessors of these families came north by covered wagon from Nebraska at the turn of the century.

working when he was horrified to feel the car lurch on its springs. A door flew open and a man leaped out. He looked big against the glare of lights from the theatre.

"What's goin' on here?" a gruff voice demanded.

Big Joe was too dumbfounded even to pull the tubes away, and when the beam of a flashlight fell on him, he stood there gaping with the cap of the gas tank plain to be seen in his hand and the smell of gasoline all about him.

"Well, blow me down!" cried the car owner. "Caught in the act, huh?" He grabbed Big Joe by the arm. "You picked the wrong car this time, fellow. I'm the town constable."

Big Joe could have broken away, perhaps, but he could never have got his team backed out. And anyway, he was still too surprised to move. Suddenly he felt metal on his wrists and found himself handcuffed. The constable played his flashlight on the tubing, the pails hanging from the reach, the drum on the democrat.

"Well, blow me down!" he growled again. Then he took the tubes out of his gas tank, dropped each in its pail and replaced the cap on his gas tank.

"Get in the rig," he ordered curtly. "And drive me round to the jail."

Two cells in the basement of the courthouse constituted the

Gas station and general store, Fenn.

town jail. Long after he was locked up in one of the cells, Big Joe could hear the booming voice of the constable telling somebody the tale.

"The missus went to the show, see, and 'long about time for her to come out, I drove down to bring her home. I was just settin' there, kind of dozin' in the car with the lights out when I seen this baby drive in beside me. Didn't pay much attention at first. But then I heard somethin' clink at the back of the car. Then I climbs out, an' there he is! Got nearly a drumful of gas, too."

The voice trailed on and on until finally Big Joe stopped listening. He began to think of Babe and Little Joe and the wheat that would not be seeded now. He went to sleep thinking, and dreamed wretchedly of pails and rubber tubing and the smell of gasoline, the taste of gasoline.

On the following morning Big Joe came up before a magistrate — a sour-faced, emaciated old man seemingly in an advanced stage of influenza. He looked as though he had wintered on Russian thistle, Big Joe thought.

The constable told his story with frequent interruptions while the magistrate sneezed or performed noisy operations with handkerchiefs. Each sneeze was a tremendous eruption which ended with an exasperated "Dammit!"

"You — ah-h-choo! Dammit! — got anything to say?" he demanded, glaring at Big Joe in a way that could only mean ten years at hard labour.

But Big Joe told his story — a plain, unvarnished story, for it was not in him to plead. He told about the granary and tractor that the wind had uncovered after five years' burial, and about his failure to get tractor fuel on credit. He told about Babe and Little Joe. He mentioned the few merchants in Sanford who knew him.

The constable, at least, seemed impressed, and whispered to the magistrate that a little investigation might be advisable. The magistrate consenting, Joe was led back to his cell with those terrific sneezes ringing in his ears.

He was not surprised when told on the following day that the magistrate had taken to his bed.

But the constable was a good egg. He spent some time consulting the merchants Big Joe had mentioned. They all gave Joe a good character. They all had refused him credit — solely on the ground that they thought it was folly to seed a crop in that south country.

One of them knew Uncle Pete.

"That old coot's a moonshiner," he said, "You can't really blame him for that. For him to do without liquor is like keepin' milk from a baby. The old so-and-so came in here last winter with a tale about their relief potatoes bein' all froze. Big Joe told me weeks later that that was a lie. But Uncle Pete got more potatoes anyway — and none of them reached home. He must have quite a cache of alcohol someplace, and I hear it's mighty good stuff, too. I've been told that Tom Dunke will buy all he can get of it."

Tom Dunke was the local bootlegger, whose business flourished as people became too poor to buy store liquor.

Late on the afternoon of the fourth day, Big Joe was haled once more before the magistrate, who seemed more emaciated than ever, and much less amiable. But, on the earnest recommendation of the constable, he finally agreed to a suspension of sentence. But he insisted obstinately on confiscation of the drum of gas for which Big Joe had risked so much.

"The man's crazy anyway," growled the magistrate. "Anybody's crazy that wants to put in another crop in that country."

"I'd like to have saved that gas for you, Joe," said the constable afterward. "I'd buy you a coupla drums myself if I had the money. Anyway, what d'ye want to stay down there for? Government experts say that country's gotta be abandoned."

"Experts, hell!" growled Joe. "I'll have maybe forty acres seeded anyway — without no more tractor fuel. If it's a good year I'll have seed for next year and somethin' to help me through the winter. I sure wish I hadn't picked on your car the other night, though."

"So do I, Joe. So do I."

He was a good egg, that constable. He paid the livery bill for Big Joe's team and sent the farmer home with a heartening slap on the back.

It was dusk when Joe arrived home — dusk of a cold, raw day with lowering, low-hanging clouds. It was not a cheerful homecoming. The thought of telling the kids that he had been in jail for stealing made Big Joe squirm. The kids thought he was a hero, kind of.

Why, once, the year before, he had heard them talking behind the house.

"What's God like?" Babe asked her brother.

And Little Joe had answered without hesitation: "He's a great big guy with a black mustache, and he smokes a pipe."

Joe himself was big and had a black mustache, and at that time he still had tobacco for his pipe.

He felt an overwhelming sense of defeat. Likely it would be a wet year. If he could have got that hundred acres sown, it would have given him a new start. But a lousy forty acres —

As he neared home he heard the barking of the tractor's exhaust. Something must have delayed Uncle Pete, so that after four days he had not finished the drum of gas yet. Tractor broke down, likely.

It was too dark to see far. He judged by the sound that the tractor was a few rods beyond the fence on Uncle Pete's place.

All at once the exhaust ceased. He heard voices — Little Joe's and Uncle Pete's.

Big Joe dropped the reins and jumped from the democrat while the tired team pricked up their ears and ambled down the road toward the gate. Big Joe crawled through the barbed wire fence.

Soon he could see the shadowy outline of the tractor. Little Joe was on the seat and Uncle Pete, in deeper shadow, was messing around in the neighbourhood of the carburetor.

"What's the matter?" called Big Joe.

"Not a drop left," wheezed Uncle Pete hoarsely.

"Hello, Pop!" shrieked Little Joe with delight. "We got the wheat seeded."

"All we got gas to see this year," agreed Big Joe despondently. "I got pinched," he added in a low voice to Uncle Pete.

"Thought so, when you didn't come home. Next day Tom Dunke came along. He'd heard about you. Heard we needed gas."

"Yeah?" Joe supposed, wearily, that everybody would hear about him, even the kids.

"He brought two drums of gas with him." Uncle Pete's voice seemed unreasonably bitter.

"Two drums of gas! What for?"

"For my — dammit — my potato licker!" gargled Uncle Pete angrily. "Wouldn't leave me a spoonful. Knew we had to have gas, see?"

"Cripes!" gasped Big Joe. "An' you got all the wheat in?"

"Ain't enough left in the drill for hen feed," Uncle Pete admitted sourly. "We just run outta gas this minute."

Big Joe was utterly overcome at the thought of Uncle Pete's self-sacrifice. He could not have been more surprised if the horses had turned from their mangers and said: "Look, Joe: You take this Russian thistle and sell it. We'll starve."

"Where's Baby?" Big Joe inquired harshly.

"She's asleep, over by the granary," Little Joe said.

"Wake her up an' bring her home."

It was almost like Uncle Pete turning his own heart's blood into the tractor's feed line. Big Joe found inadequate words.

"God bless you, Pete," he growled.

Uncle Pete's reply was not gracious, nor yet sufficiently intelligible to call profane.

A sudden clamour arose from the direction of the granary — angry shrieks from Babe, shrill answers from Little Joe.

"What's the matter?" cried Big Joe, racing towards the cries.

He seized Babe in his arms. She was wrapped in Uncle Pete's ragged sheepskin, the sleeves of which hung to her feet. Her grimy little face was white in the gloom.

"What'sa matter, Baby?"

"He spit on me!" she cried petulantly. "Little Joe did. My face is wet."

"I didn't neither," Little Joe protested.

"Now, now, Baby!"

Suddenly, Big Joe held out a hand wonderingly. Then he swept off his battered hat and turned his face up to the skies.

"It ain't spit, Baby," he said. "It's rain!"

As if they had waited for that dramatic moment, the scattered preliminary drops increased on the instant to a downpour, thudding into the soft earth, pattering on the exposed part of the newly resurrected granary. They stood in it, breathless, faces upturned. Big Joe took it as an omen.

The drought was over!

When Uncle Pete slouched up out of the gloom, it was getting wetter by the minute. But for Uncle Pete there was still a dry spell in prospect.

— from *Especially Babe* (1978) and reprinted courtesy Tree Frog Press of Edmonton.

Cliff Robinson, *Alberta Scene, ca.* 1942, linocut.

# BLUE SKIES

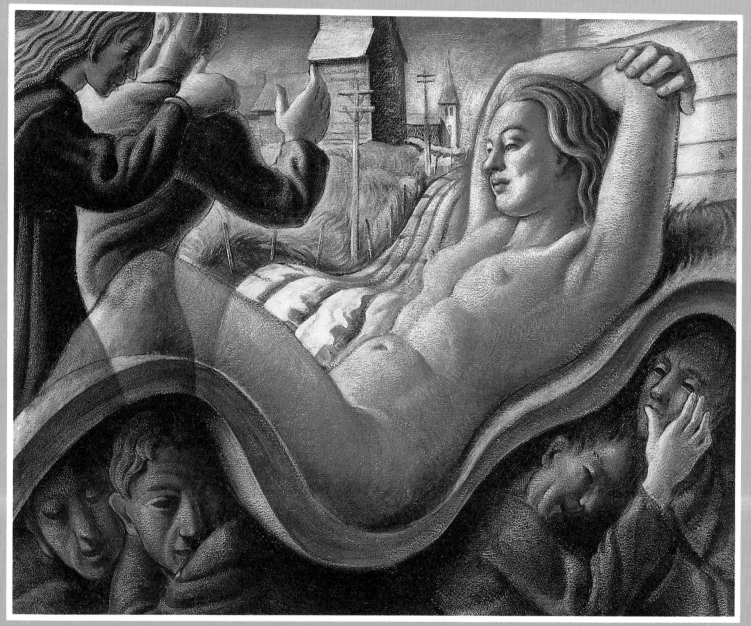

H. G. Glyde, *She Sat upon a Hill above the City, ca.* 1939, oil.

Rider, Calgary Stampede Parade.

# THE TRAVELLING NUDE

by

Henry Kreisel

## I

The only thing about the whole affair that worries me a bit is how I am going to explain to my father why I threw up a good job. My father is a very unimaginative man, and I know he has been brooding about me for a long time. Now when he hears about the travelling nude, he's quite likely to become momentarily deranged. But that, I'm afraid, can't be helped.

Ever since the subject was first broached and the debate got passionate, splitting at least one husband and wife right down the middle, I've had a very distinct impression of her. I admit it's quite ludicrous, but you'll admit (though my father isn't likely to) that it has a certain kind of charm.

There she is. Quite good-looking. Not anything spectacular, you understand. The pay is hardly good enough to attract anything like that, and the conditions of work are not exactly first class. There's a lot of travelling involved, and the work has to be done mostly in small towns, pop. 1275 or 1423, and she has to stay in rather dingy hotels, even though these hotels have fancy names, like the *Ritz* or the *Imperial*. But she has a pretty good figure, nonetheless. Nicely proportioned. Breasts pretty firm, though perhaps now beginning to droop a little, with the first flush of youth departed. A bit of a fatty fold starting to show round her middle. But the buttocks still firm, and the thighs round and full, and the legs long and shapely. A good nude, take it all in all. Now she goes to all these little places, pop. 1500 and less, a different place each week, and wherever she goes (my father is going to find this hard to understand) she travels in the nude. She wears nothing except a pair of high-heeled shoes. Even in the winter when it's very cold. She's a travelling nude, you see. And she travels out of Edmonton, Alta., pop. 250,000 or so, a fair-sized city.

She takes a taxi from the house she rooms in (that's part of allowable expenses) to either the C.P.R. or C.N.R. or Greyhound Bus Station, and there she gets out, proud, head held high, but she's very demure and a bit shy at the same time. So with a nonchalantly grand manner she tips the taxi driver ten cents and walks into the station. He's a bit pop-eyed, and so are most of the other people, but I never worry very much about their reaction. She's accepted, more or less. She's known as the travelling nude and that's all there is to it.

Sometimes, in the winter, I feel I'd like to drape a warm coat around her, but I resist this impulse. She's a hardy soul. She can stand the cold. Anyway, there she goes. Oh, I forgot to tell you. She also carries a handbag. She is, after all, a woman.

So she traipses up to the ticket window, and says (her voice is husky, in a feminine, though not exactly seductive way), "One ticket, return, to Great Fish Lake, please." Or it might be Three Bear Hills, or Pollux, or Castor, or any number of other places, for she is constantly kept busy for eight or nine months of the year. And then she rummages about in her capacious handbag, pays for her ticket, looks somewhat disapprovingly at the astonished clerk who gapes wide-eyed at her slightly drooping breasts (the first flush of youth now gone), not knowing whether to be scandalized or erotically aroused, and then walks over to the newsstand and buys, as is her custom, a copy of the *Ladies' Home Journal* or *Chatelaine* or *Vogue*, for she must know what the well-dressed woman wears this season, or what Dr. Blatz or Dr. Spock thinks this month about the psyche of the pre-school child, or what delicious dishes can be concocted this week out of last Sunday's left-over roast. She is a well-informed nude, you see, garnering up bits of useful information as she travels by train or bus.

So she arrives at last in Great Fish Lake, or Three Bear Hills, or Castor, or Pollux, and gets off the bus or the train, and the stationmaster and the local inhabitants look at each other knowingly and say, "Oh, here goes the travelling nude. Guess there's going to be a great deal of activity over at the Community Hall tonight," and they smile and wink broadly at each other, but look very soberly as she walks past them, and doff their hats and say, "Good afternoon, ma'm. Not too cold for you, I hope," and she smiles back graciously, showing as she does so a gap (unfortunate blemish!) in the upper row of her teeth.

And the desk-clerk at the *Great Fish Lake Imperial* or the *Three Bear Hills Ritz*, wooden buildings, once painted white, with name emblazoned in black block letters, looks down the main street and sees her coming, and says to a man drowsing in a sagging, brown, cracked leather chair, "There's the travelling nude. That means the old Community Hall is going to be all lit up tonight," and winks at the man in the sagging chair, who rouses himself with a startled snore and looks at her as she walks towards the hotel, balancing delicately on her high-heeled shoes, her handbag now slung across her shoulder.

The desk-clerk has her key ready. "Same room as last time, ma'm. 14A." The number 13 is delicately skipped at the *Great Fish Lake Imperial* or the *Three Bear Hills Ritz*.

She smiles her gap-toothed smile, thanks him, and taking her key, walks up the stairs, and the two men look thoughtfully at her firm buttocks swaying lightly from side to side as she

Ralph Tucker, 83, Endiang. He and his brother first came to the Hand Hills Stampede in 1918 where they boasted they could ride "anything with hair on it."

Hutterites watch the annual Pincher Creek Rodeo Parade.

Dancers, Calgary Stampede Parade.

mounts to the first floor and lets herself into her room.

Once in, she sighs deeply and lies down on her bed. A long evening's work now stretches before her, and she does not anticipate it with particular pleasure. The work is tiring, and she feels tired already, even before it's begun, for she's no longer quite as energetic as she once was.

Evening comes. A few street lights in the main street go on, and the gray-haired, mustachioed caretaker gets everything ready, and then, singly or in groups, they begin to emerge from the small houses in the unlit streets or from farmhouses further away, making their way on foot or in cars that bump along rutty roads, and so at last converge upon the Community Hall, and, carrying satchels and sundry other equipment, greet each other and go into the Hall and sit down busily on chairs arranged in a wide semi-circle, and now, talking to each other, they wait. There are pinched-looking women, resigned to spinsterhood, and middle-aged matrons, their child-rearing task now done; there are a few youngish couples, and two or three single men.

"Are we all here?" says a cheerful female voice. "Good. Now we must really work tonight. She'll be here in a minute. Take advantage of your opportunity. Remember, she won't be here for another six months or so."

Out of the satchels come sheets of drawing paper and charcoal pencils, and they all sit there, poised, expectant, ready for action.

The door opens and with stately steps, head held high, her bearing almost regal, the travelling nude enters, makes her way smiling, as if bestowing royal grace, to a chair in the middle of the semi-circle and sits down. Her work has now begun.

"Now, class," says the cheerful female, who teaches in the local elementary school during the day, "tonight we'll try and draw the sitting nude. Tomorrow we'll draw the nude standing, and the day after that the reclining nude. I hope you'll all be here again then, for as Mr. Mahler told us, we cannot become painters without learning to draw the human figure exactly, can we now?" And smiles all round the semi-circle, and then nods pleasantly at the sitting travelling nude.

The travelling nude arranges herself on her chair, trying to make herself as comfortable as possible. She now seems oblivious of the faces staring at her. Each face now sees her from its own angle. There is a pause while each drinks in the vision of "Figure. Female. Sitting. Nude." At last they begin to sketch away, now satisfied, now frustrated; erase, start again;

look over their shoulders to see what their neighbors are doing, while all the while the cheerful female circulates among them, admonishing, guiding, calling on the team to give their all. "Be sure and remember that Mr. Mahler comes next month," she cries, "and that we want to show him that we've really been making progress."

So for three evenings they sketch the travelling nude until their creative energies are quite exhausted, their paper all used up, their pencils blunt.

Early in the morning, on the fourth day after her arrival, the travelling nude departs. She is glad the work for this week is over, looks forward to lounging about for a few days in Edmonton. She is quite tired, for the accommodation is dingy, the food stale and steamy, and the work is strenuous, exhausting even. And yet she knows that in the following week she will set out again and spend three days in some little town to help along the growth of culture in the land.

## II

Perhaps it would be better if I made up some commonplace story and never said anything at all about the travelling nude to my father. For if I told him the truth, I would only succeed in calling forth his Job-like posture. On such occasions he sighs deeply, lifts his head towards the ceiling of the room, as if God sat there in a corner, rolls his eyes, and spreads his arms out wide, resigned to his martyrdom. "Everybody has some cross to bear," he told me once. "You are my cross." I'm sure he thinks I am mad.

It occurs to me that you might think so, too. Let me assure you that I am as sane as you. I am an artist. My name is Herman O. Mahler. I am aware that "Mahler" is the German word for painter. So perhaps long ago one of my ancestors was a painter, and the thought that this familial talent, after lying dormant for many generations, burst forth again and manifested itself in me, makes me quite excited, creating a bond between me and that remote ancestor whose name proclaimed his art. My father sneered at the notion. So far as he knew or cared to admit the Mahlers were all respectable businessmen, ever since the first Canadian Mahler, my grandfather, established a general store in Orillia, a small Ontario town. I myself was born in Toronto twenty-seven years ago.

When I announced my intention of becoming a painter, my father stormed up and down our living room, crying incessantly,

"Why did I slave all these years? For what? For what? What was the point? What?"

I, for my part, kept on saying, "I don't see any logical connection here," but he merely repeated, "Why did I slave all these years? For what? For what?"

My mother didn't take any of this seriously. She thought my ambition would burn itself out. I was only seventeen at the time. But when the flames burned even lustier, my mother, who is a realistic woman, persuaded my father to let me go to the Ontario College of Art.

He looked the place over and was quite impressed by its size and general air of stolidity. As he put it to my mother, "The building is beautiful. Big solid pillars. Good stone. Nice trees all around. And the inside, too. Respectable. Quiet. Clean. Not like those attics you hear about. Well, maybe there's something to this art business after all."

I studied at the Ontario College of Art for three years, learned to draw "Figure. Female. Reclining. Nude." "Figure. Female. Sitting. Nude." Learned to work in oil, tempera, and various other media, took several courses in the history of art, and emerged at last a duly certified Mahler.

By the time I was twenty-four or twenty-five I had already passed through several well-recognizable periods. My first period was the blue period, and it is astonishing what nuances of blue I could produce. My style then was generally realistic, although my father, on seeing one of my paintings, exclaimed, "Blue horses! Why, that's impossible! Who ever saw a blue horse?"

I moved on to my pink period and painted in pink more or less the same subjects which I had hitherto painted in blue. "Pink horses!" my father exclaimed. "Why, that's impossible! Who ever saw a pink horse?"

I moved rapidly on to my Cubist period, in which I produced at least one remarkable painting, a largish oil, entitled, "Nude Descending Staircase," which practically caused my father to suffer an apoplexy and to mutter darkly about fraud and the corruption of the young. It was the title that annoyed him, for he could recognize no nude in the picture itself. My mother contented herself with a clicking of her tongue and a modest statement that these things were beyond her.

After my Cubist period came my Abstract period, and at last I felt that I had found my style. Here imagination was not restricted. I felt free, with all nature at my feet. I was a conqueror. Neither space nor time could now contain me. My father was now quite certain that I was mad.

In five years of painting I sold paintings totalling two hundred dollars, and even my poor mathematical brain managed to compute that this amounted to only forty dollars per annum. What was most irksome, however, was the fact that since I continued to live at home and was therefore in a manner of speaking a kept man, my father, who was after all doing the keeping, felt himself entitled to keep up a consistent, sniping, carping sort of criticism about the noble art of painting in general and my own activity in particular. He wondered why this curse had been wished on his only son, for whom he had envisaged a bright and rosy future in the retailing business. The idea that I was carrying on the tradition established by a remote Mahler he dismissed with contempt.

At last he began to insist that I earn my own living. What was I to do? I refused to prostitute my original, God-given talent, for I felt that if I did so I would in some obscure way be betraying the honor and integrity of that remote Mahler who had passed on his mantle to me and was now watching to see what I would do with it. Imagine my joy, therefore, when I read in an art magazine that the Extension Department of the University of Alberta was looking for an Extension lecturer in art, whose business it would be to travel the length and breadth of the province and give a series of short courses (none longer than a week) in various small towns. What marvellous vistas opened up before me! I would be a true servant of the noble art of painting. What hidden talents I would discover, what rough diamonds I would unearth, polish and present to the world! And I would go on painting myself. Thus I could pursue the noble art to which I had dedicated myself and keep on eating at the same time without relying on the charity of my father or prostituting the inner me.

I applied for the job and was duly appointed.

### III

I resigned from this position largely because of the travelling nude.

I must be frank. The rough diamonds I hoped to find turned out to be chunks of coal. And not even coal of the first grade, either. But they were most pleasant pieces of coal, kind and most appreciative. I became known in the little towns and in the pokey hotels, and held forth in sundry Community Halls

on the elements of the noble art of painting as taught in the Ontario College of Art. Thus is the light spread into the furthermost corners of the land.

Most of my students were unfortunately wholly intent on reproducing mountains and lakes and flowers with a passion that depressed me. "More imagination!" I cried. "Use all the imagination you have!" Whereupon dear Mrs. McGregor, when next I arrived in her neck of the woods, showed proudly a canvas on which she had painted a desert sheik, in long white robes and red fez, sitting in a posture meant to be majestic on an improbable-looking Arabian horse, and staring at what was unquestionably a frozen lake in front of him, and the snow-capped Rocky Mountains ringing him all round. The critical mind stood awed and aghast. All I could mutter was, "You could improve the folds in the sheik's robe."

I did not despair. My earnest hope was to guide my charges away from nature and lead them, via the human figure, to the glory and perfect freedom of Abstraction. I began first by having one or another of my students pose, and I showed them how a face could be broken down into its geometrical components. It was rather more difficult to demonstrate how the clothed body could so be broken down, and it was in Three Bear Hills that I made the fatal remark.

"What we need for a real study of the human figure," I said, "is someone to model for us in the nude."

Well, the ice descended on the Three Bear Hills Community Hall. Shocked looks crissed and crossed, and dear Mrs. McGregor looked at me with infinite pain, as if to say, "You wouldn't surely mean me?"

I found myself shaking my head and mumbling, "No. No. That is not what I meant at all," when suddenly there was the unmistakable gravel voice of Thomas Cullen breaking the icy silence with a loud "Hear! Hear!"

I turned to look at him, and there he was, as sprightly a sixty-year-old as ever you saw, small and wiry, with a little bald-pated head, looking straight at Nancy Hall, a fair to middling thirty-year-old blossoming bud, and "Hear! Hear!" he cried again. "That's what we need alright."

"Shame!" cried dear Mrs. McGregor. "Shame!"

"For academic purposes merely," said Thomas Cullen saucily.

"Shame!" cried Mrs. McGregor again. "Shame!"

I managed to smooth things over, but the fertile seed continued to sprout in Thomas Cullen's bald-pated head and the

A job for the whole family, Millarville Fair.

Prize ram, Millarville.

*Opposite:*
Keith Winter and goose, Millarville.

following June bore glorious fruit in Medicine Hat.

Once a year there is a meeting of the Community Art Classes in one of the larger centres, and whoever has the time gathers there for a shindig lasting a day. There are discussions in small groups about how things could be improved and then all the students exhibit their pictures, and in the evening there's a banquet and there's a guest speaker, and afterwards the group chairmen present a series of resolutions and everybody votes on them, and then, in a softly-glowing mood of togetherness and comradeship the group dissolves, thinking that the art of painting has been truly and nobly served.

As leader and travelling mentor I was expected to arrange this annual event, and things went pretty smoothly. That ancient Mahler might have thought the guild of medieval painters had been miraculously revived, until, of course, he'd seen the paintings. After the discussions and the exhibition we all gathered in the banqueting room of a restaurant, and sat on hard, narrow chairs around long tables, eating tough chicken and soggy boiled potatoes and dried-out cole slaw. After the dessert, I rapped a teaspoon against a glass and introduced our guest speaker, a nice enough fellow who'd come out of Edmonton at my request, and who now began to warble about the aesthetics of modern art, and threw names about, like Leger, and Braque, and Mondrian, and Picasso, and everybody nodded knowingly, feeling cultured and really dead centre, if you know what I mean. At last he finished warbling and sat down amid polite applause.

The next item on the agenda was "Resolutions." It's funny, but I can never even think of the word "resolution" without at once seeing a wastepaper basket. I guess that is what Freud meant by free association. A procession of wastepaper baskets now began to march through my head as our little band of devotees resolved in various ways to make the cultural desert bloom.

It was getting pretty hot and my chair seemed to be getting smaller and smaller, and just as I thought we were all done, there was the loud clearing of a throat, and Thomas Cullen cried out, "I have another resolution, Mr. Chairman."

Another wastepaper basket strutted slowly through my head. "But," I said, "you didn't chair one of the groups, did you, Mr. Cullen?"

"No," said Thomas Cullen, "I did not. This is a private resolution." He cleared his throat again and took a sip of water. Then he got up, straightened his tie, reached deep into the inner recesses of his breast-pocket and brought out a piece of paper.

"Inasmuch and because no painter can call himself a painter unless he knows the anatomy of the human figure," Thomas Cullen read solemnly, "and inasmuch as it is impossible to study and know the human figure unless that figure is nude, be it therefore resolved that the authorities in question secure a travelling nude who would go from community to community. . . . "

Thomas Cullen had more to say, but I didn't hear it. For, like Venus rising from the waves, the travelling nude rose in my mind, fully fashioned, although with the first flush of youth now gone.

The next voice I heard distinctly was that of Mr. Edward Nash, who sat next to his wife, and who now said loudly and clearly, "I second the motion."

His wife turned on him with a startled look that froze on her face and gave me some idea of what Sodom and Gomorrah must have been like. "You wouldn't," she hissed. "You wouldn't."

"I second Mr. Cullen's motion," said Edward Nash stoutly. "A travelling nude — that's what we need to perfect ourselves as painters."

"You men!" said Mrs. Nash indignantly. "You're all alike. Painters, indeed! Travelling nudes! Mountains and horses are good enough to practice on."

"I'm sure the gentlemen are acting from highest motives," I said, trying to soften things up.

"Lowest motives," cried Mrs. McGregor, "if you ask me."

"Now, now," I said sternly. "Let's have an orderly debate."

"I don't see what there is to debate," said Mrs. Nash. "Lechery. That's all."

In the far corner portly Mr. Barrhead rose. He was about fifty, and he specialized in painting lakes. He was, I believe, a lawyer. "There's some merit in the resolution before us," he began. "However, the whole thing is premature. Our fellow citizens would undoubtedly misconstrue this — this business, and the Community Art Classes would likely get a bad name. In fact, this thing would likely kill the whole development."

"I disagree emphatically, Mr. Chairman," protested Thomas Cullen. "If we get a travelling nude it would be the biggest shot in the arm that painting ever got in this province."

It was at this moment that I saw the travelling nude demurely walk to the hotel in her high-heeled shoes, and I was so

The 70th annual Hand Hills Stampede, June 11, 1986. The first
event was organized by Jack Miller to provide aid for the Red Cross
in their work for the wounded in World War I.

William Panko, *Rodeo*, ca. 1935, watercolour.

engrossed in my vision that I missed most of what followed, though Mrs. Nash threw herself into the battle with renewed vigor and her voice dominated all.

"Question!" someone shouted. "Question!"

"Before we vote," cried Thomas Cullen, obviously trying desperately to save his resolution, "let's ask Mr. Mahler what he thinks."

The noise subsided. All turned to me.

"I think it's an excellent idea," I said firmly. "If there's anything you people need more than anything else it's a travelling nude."

"You can't mean that," cried Mrs. Nash after a moment of stunned silence.

"I do," I said firmly, for my mind was filled with the vision I had seen.

"I knew it," cried Mrs. McGregor. "I knew it all the time." I have often wondered since what exactly it was that Mrs. McGregor knew.

The vote was taken. Fifty-two against, and one for. Mr. Edward Nash half-raised his hand to vote "aye", but after a quick look at his furious spouse, he dropped it again, and abstained.

IV

It was about two weeks after this memorable scene that my boss in Edmonton summoned me to his office. He's a very nice fellow, though more interested in oil wells than in oil paint, and our relations had always been pleasant enough.

"Ah, Mahler," he greeted me. "It's good to see you. Sit down." He was sucking on a pipe and began to rummage about for something on his desk. "Everything all right?" he asked casually.

"Fine," I said. "Everything's fine. One more trip to Three Bear Hills and other points South, and that's it for this year. Thank God."

He gave me a quick look. "Why 'Thank God'?" he asked. "Aren't you happy in your work?"

"Oh, sure," I said. "But I'm...."

"Quite so," he interrupted. "Quite so." It was quite obvious that he wasn't really much interested. He was filling his pipe and lighting it, and in between puffs he said, "I called you in, Mahler, because of this," and he held up a letter that he had unearthed from a pile on his desk. "It's nothing," he said nonchalantly. "I'm sure you can explain."

I was getting a bit annoyed, I must admit. If it was nothing, then what was there to explain?

A father watches his daughter compete in the Barrel Races, Hand Hills.

Chuckwagon Races, Hand Hills.

Loosening up for the Saddle Bronc Riding Competition, Hand Hills.

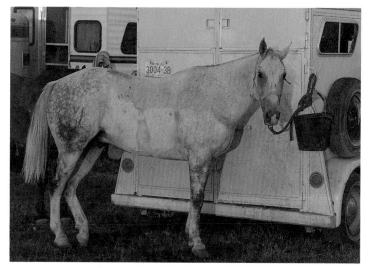

Horse and trailer, High River.

"It's a complaint," he said. "Signed by about fifteen of your students. I think it's a joke or something. But it appears that you are strongly in favor of a travelling nude."

I looked him straight in the eye. "That's right," I said. "It's got to the point where you can't have any kind of development of the community art classes unless you get a travelling nude. And the sooner the better." I leaned forward and tapped my knuckles on his desk for emphasis.

"You're not serious," he said.

"I was never more serious in my life," I said. "And what's more, we need the kind of nude that'll really travel in the nude."

"You're not serious," he said again, incredulously. His pipe went out and he sucked on it desperately.

"Furthermore," I continued, quite reckless now, "unless we get a travelling nude, I can't possibly continue to instruct here. I'm sick and tired of mountains and lakes. Our students have to be initiated into the secrets of female, figure, sitting, nude."

"Mahler!" he said, and there was alarm in his voice, "you must be mad."

"Drink deep or taste not the Pierian spring," I said.

"Mahler!" he cried. "What the. . . ."

"The original resolution called for the authorities to secure a travelling nude," I informed him calmly. " 'Authorities' in this case means you. So if I were you, I'd start advertising."

"Mahler," he said. His hands were trembling, and he put his pipe down on his desk. "Please go and see a doctor."

"I will not be insulted," I said haughtily. "I have my artistic pride. It runs in the family. You will have my letter of resignation in the morning."

I left him speechless, poor fellow. I think deep down I must have wanted to give up this job. Don't you?

Oh, I forgot to tell you. The name of the travelling nude was Valerie. She had no surname. Or if she did, I never knew it.

# STAMPEDE

## JACK MILLER'S RANCH
### Sec. 12-29-16, Handhills Lake

HANNA HERALD STUDIOS

## Friday, July 20th, 1917

FOR EXCLUSIVE BENEFIT OF RED CROSS

The Greatest Programme of Wild-Western Events, Staged North of the **Red Deer**, **East** of Calgary.

Harold W. McCrea, untitled, 1917.

# MEMORIES

The family of the photographer, Elliot Barnes, on the Green Spot, hand tinted by Carole Harmon.
(Whyte Museum of the Canadian Rockies, Collection of Elliot Barnes.)

Elliot Barnes was an American writer, sportsman, and photographer, who immigrated to Canada in 1905 to ranch on the Kootenay Plains. (Archives of the Canadian Rockies, Banff.)

A happy ending for everyone in the 1920 movie "Sergeant Cameron of the Mounted." (Whyte Museum of the Canadian Rockies, Banff.)

The famous country singer, Wilf Carter, serenades a small circle of friends, *ca*. 1936. (Whyte Museum of the Canadian Rockies, Banff. Collection of the Canadian Pacific Railway.)

A moment of reflection at Bow Lake in 1924. (Whyte Museum of the Canadian Rockies. Byron Harmon Collection.)

Philmaster Proctor on the shore of Maligne Lake, Alpine Club of Canada—Smithsonian Robson Expedition, 1911. (Whyte Museum of the Canadian Rockies. Byron Harmon Collection.)

Byron Harmon naps and a friend reads while they wait for the sun to break through clouds over the Ramparts near Amethyst Lake in 1918. Harmon was a well-known and prolific photographer of the Rockies. (Whyte Museum of the Canadian Rockies.)

Seventeen climbers silhouetted at the foot of Yoho Glacier in about 1914. (Whyte Museum of the Canadian Rockies. Byron Harmon Collection.)

In 1907 members of the Alpine Club of Canada pose for the camera near the Giant Steps, Paradise Valley. (Whyte Museum of the Canadian Rockies. Collection of Byron Harmon.)

Pete Brewster and Howard O'Hagan. (Collection of Joe Weiss.)

Caribou above Maligne Lake. (Collection of Joe Weiss.)

Conrad Kain, one of Canada's greatest climbers, leads a party on Resplendent Mountain in 1915. (Whyte Museum of the Canadian Rockies. Byron Harmon Collection.)

*Opposite:*
Glacier. (Collection of Joe Weiss.)

# TRAILBLAZING

Carl Rungius, *Crossing The Stream, ca.* 1920, oil on canvas. One of Jimmy Simpson's guides, Harry Lang, leads a pack train across Bear Creek.

Looking south from Mountain Park.

# THE WHITE HORSE

by
Howard O'Hagan

When a man is packing in the mountains it is a good rule to have in his outfit a white horse. In the evening, at the end of the day's travel, the horses are turned loose to graze and at sun-up the packer goes out on foot to drive them in to camp. A white horse can be seen far away on a side hill or among the willows on the flats or showing for a moment deep in the timber when the bays, roans, blacks, or buck-skins, making up the rest of the bunch, stand hidden. Without having to follow tracks, to listen for the always elusive sound of a bell, the packer sees at once where some, at least, of his horses are, rounds them up, and brings them in.

Yet on the morning that Nick Durban decided that his white packhorse, Bedford, was lost, this very whiteness was a disadvantage. It was in early March, and windless, after a snowfall. Nick's cabin, from which in the winters he trapped, was on a rise above the forks of the Little Hay, between the foothills and the first range of the Rockies. As he stood on his snowshoes outside its door, bundled in mackinaw jacket and trousers, beaver cap, moose-hide mitts, and moccasins, snow was everywhere about him. It was on the branches of the pine trees and on the spruce and balsam high upon the mountain sides. It lay heavy on the ice-filled creek and spread white and dazzling across the meadows, bright enough to blister the eyes. The whole world, it appeared to Nick, must be one white ball whirling around the silver sun. A white horse would melt into it like a handful of flour. His bones, flesh, and hair would dissolve, would perish, would be absorbed by the translucent day.

The tracks Bedford had made had been filled in by fresh snow, dusted over by the wind and for a week he had not been in his lean-to shelter against the cabin where Nick, on the other side of the log wall, could hear his warm breathing and the crunch of his hooves on the frosty ground. But until now, the fourth morning that, neglecting his marten traps, he had set out to look for the white horse, Nick had assured himself that Bedford was not lost. He had merely strayed. In his search, extending over those four days, Nick had circled the meadows, followed the creeks to their head, and returned in the late afternoons, his snowshoe trail stretching like a pattern of lace from his feet, and from his door in the morning seen again the cold mist lying in the draws, as if it were his breath left there the previous day in his passing.

Only one place remained to him to go — the bench directly behind above the cabin, six miles distant beyond muskeg and brule. It was called the High Valley for some reason that Nick could never understand for it was no more than a sloping tangle of jack-pine and down-timber.

Yet, on the whole, poor though the name might be, he was glad that it had one. It was more home-like and warmer to have names about. In the valley only the creek was named and one mountain, called Black Mountain. All the hills were nameless. Even the pass which Nick crossed several times a year, leading into town and the railroad, was without a proper name. On the town side it was known as the "pass to the Little Hay" and on its north side the few trappers and homesteaders who used it, referred to it as the "pass to town". The matter had been discussed between Nick and his good friend Olaf, the Swede, who ran a trapline farther down the Little Hay. Olaf had said that in the old country all such places had names, but he did not see how, in these foothills a pass, especially a low, gentle pass, that had no name, would acquire one.

The High Valley — that was different. It had had a name longer than anyone could remember, and it was up there that the white horse, wandering from the cabin, might have gone for shelter or to rustle food. Nick, crossing the meadow from his cabin, now climbed up after him, snow boiling about his legs, his snowshoes sunk in the snow until he seemed to be walking on his knees. It was very cold. The air scorched his nostrils, his breath hissed from his lips, and icicles hung from his grey moustache and beaded upon his brows.

He saw wolf tracks — five sets of them, a litter hunting with their dam and farther on a moose had broken trail for him up a tilted forest aisle.

As he went along he recalled trips he and Bedford had made together when they both were young and, looking back, those years were green, the valleys green, veined with sparkling streams of water, and in them grass grew bunched and strong and thick . . . . His memory took him as far as the early days when the railroad came to the mountains. It was at that time, about 1908, that Nick had set himself up as a packer. He had had his own string of horses and packed supplies to a survey camp from Edson at the end of steel in Alberta. He packed through the foothills into the Athabaska valley, up against the Rocky Mountains where the blue glaciers glimmered. Sometimes when he had dumped his loads and unsaddled his horses, the surveyor, a Mr. Bedford, asked him into his tent for a glass of whiskey.

Mr. Bedford — Nick doubted that he had a first name — was a tall, spare Englishman from between whose sallow cheeks a sharp, red nose showed as a chronic inflammation. Often, coming in from the wind, his eyes watered, as if, in truth, it pained him. Each day after his work on the line, Mr. Bedford, returning to camp, removed his soiled clothes and took a bath in a tin tub made ready for him on the creek bank. Then he dressed in a black suit, white shirt and black bow tie, silk socks, and patent leather shoes and walked forth and back before his tent, polishing his eyeglasses, whose long, black ribbon was looped about his neck. He ate his supper, brought by the chainman (who had already filled his bathtub), the youngest member of the party, off a folding table covered with white oilcloth and put by his tent door. All of this impressed Nick as an unqualified achievement for a man living under canvas. The detail upon which afterwards he had most remarked, however, was the silk handkerchief Mr. Bedford on these occasions wore tucked up his sleeve. Until then Nick had seen only two things come out of a sleeve — a hand, and, now and again, a card.

It was following this year's work that his bay mare dropped the dappled colt, which as the years passed was to turn white and to which, in tribute to their association, Nick gave Mr. Bedford's name. The colt was long in the leg, high withered, with one blue eye. After his weaning he developed into a solitary beast, feeding a bit away from the herd on the side hill, a habit which finally determined his naming.

In time, Mr. Bedford and the other surveyors concluded their tasks and went away. The railroad hammered its way along the trail they had blazed. Soon trains howled through the Athabasca valley. Nick, resenting the intrusion, drew back into the northern hills, built his cabin, and laid out his trapline. For a while he kept his six head of horses, using them on hunting trips in the fall. As the years passed, these long trips became less frequent. His horses fell away. One of them he sold to a homesteader over the divide. One of them the wolves ran down. The others foundered in the snow, or purged with new spring grass, lay down in weakness and failed to rise from some south-facing hollow.

At last only Bedford remained. Foaled in the foothills, he outlived the others brought in from the plains. Nick was able to remember it was thirty years, half a lifetime, since Bedford had been a colt. They had grown old side by side, but it seemed that the white horse had aged two years to his one, so that now, at thirty, he was about to leave off where his owner, as a packer, had begun.

For Bedford, probably the oldest horse on the Athabasca watershed — Nick knew of no other surviving from construction days — had not been worked for many years. He had been loose to graze. With age his joints had stiffened and his tendons could be heard snapping when he walked. Usually he stayed close at hand — the feed was good and he had had it all to himself — dozing in the sun or under the shed built for him against the cabin. From long standing the horn of his hooves grew long, forcing him back on his fetlocks. His teeth had worn down and long pieces of grass and even of willow showed in his dung, swallowed whole and passed undigested.

By those dried piles of dung, found along the creek or on a gravel bar in the creek or in the willows where the horse had gone to escape the flies or among the timber where the rain or wind had urged him, Nick more than once had paused to shake his head, part in dismay and part in anger. They gave him hurt within his entrails, as if the failure, of which they were evidence, were his own. Age was the portion shared by him with the white horse. It was age which over the period of years had cut down the length of his trapline from eighty miles to sixty, from sixty to forty, from forty to thirty, until now on his weekly rounds, he travelled only twenty miles to clean his traps.

They had come a long journey together — yet the horse, whose wants foretold the journey's end, was at the same time the one abiding link with its beginning, with the early days, with youth, when Nick, in a crimson shirt rode at the head of his pack outfit and drank whiskey with Mr. Bedford and climbed all day hunting and never knew what it was to have to stop for breath on a hill slope or to be tired coming into camp with a haunch of meat over his shoulder.

More recently there had been the trips into town with the fur catch. Nick did not ride Bedford. Bedford was a pack horse and had not been broken to ride and now he was too old to pack. Nick packed the fur on his own back. He saddled the white horse and led him with a fancy Indian bridle over the pass and down the thirty miles of trail, taken in easy stages, to the railroad. Some people laughed at that. In town the boys threw stones, shouting that the old man was afraid to ride the old horse. Nick spat on the rutted road, shook his fist at them.

Train conductor, Jasper Station.

Cyndi Smith, patrolwoman with Parks Canada Warden Service, on the Astoria Trail into the Tonquin Valley.

After all, a man with self-respect did not go to town without a horse, or bring his horse in naked, or try to break to ride a horse as old as Bedford.

Afterwards, were the summer evenings at the cabin on the Little Hay. At supper Bedford put his head through the open window, shutting out the sunset, bringing an early dusk indoors. His flaring nostrils blew crumbs from the table top or he gathered up with his awkward lips the oatmeal spread there for him or nibbled at a piece of bannock set out to cool. Sometimes he nuzzled the tobacco can, which held sugar, and upset it. They had had words over that. Nick had even raised his voice. Then Bedford withdrew, walking stiffly down to the meadow where, belly deep in grass, he looked up and nickered.

The sun had passed its height when Nick, climbing through the snow from his cabin, pausing every few minutes to draw wind, now came upon him in the High Valley. Bedford was in a clump of second-growth jack-pine, their trunks laced with old, fallen logs, as securely corralled as he had ever been. His lower jaw had dropped, showing the yellow discs of his teeth and, though one ear was cocked, his blue eye was glazed and drowsy. Robed and bearded with snow, he sat on his haunches, his shoulder leaned against a tree. His gaunt rib cage bulged, the ribs wide-spaced with his years, and standing beside him, Nick kicked at a white mound pile of dung. The horse had been caught there for some days, nibbling at bark and dry twigs, too weak to paw down to the scarce, pale grass or yet to force his way out over the down timber. The cold had hamstrung him and his back legs had collapsed. He was frozen stiff and solid.

Nick slipped his hands from the mitts which, suspended by a cord from around his neck, fell and slapped against his thighs. He stepped forward and while with his right hand he patted the horse's withers, trying to smooth the rigid, upstanding fur, and pinched the gristle under the roots of the mane, he held his left hand, cupped as with sugar or oatmeal up to the mouth, against the chill, breathless nostrils. Snow dropped from the horse's mane into rounded, silent pits by his snowshoes. The snow lay around Bedford, lapping at his flanks, like a slow and ever rising flood. It lay over all the hills and all the mountains, deeper and heavier than a man had thought for, farther than his eyes had ever seen. Nick walked upon it on his snowshoes and beneath its surface Bedford was already sinking. On it the sun threw their shadows, merged them in a dark and inky

pool. He put his head closer to the horse. He said a word and went away, downhill over the broken trail to his cabin, settling his webbed feet with care, aware of the depths which sustained them.

After a time, crossing a creek bed, he stood to listen, hearing water under the ice beneath his snowshoes, pulsing against his foot soles. He waited, attentive to the soft, lively sound of spring. Here, lower in the valley, it had thawed at noonday and now at evening a light crust had formed on the snow. Later, when he could already see the fork of the valley, and up to his left the pass to town, the pass without a name, Nick heard very clearly and near to him the clang of a bell, as though a horse, sheltered by the spruce tree over yonder, had tossed his head. He went on, knowing that no horse bell was within a hundred miles and that a man, alone, heard what he most wants to hear.

Before entering his cabin, he hesitated at the foot of the rise on which it rested measuring again its lines and worth. It was a well-built cabin, logs securely housed and chinked, roof dry and firm beneath the burden of snow. It would last a long time yet, beaten by the drifts upon its hill top.

In the cabin Nick lit the lantern and hung it from the beam. Making a fire in the stove, he went over to his bunk and rolled back the blankets and mattress revealing the old newspapers he had put there to keep out the draft. They were the back pages, the pages of the want-ads, for experience had taught him that their close-set type was the warmest. Headlines let in the air. Here among the little words, where men sought jobs, offered their small goods for sale, made inquiry for friends and relatives and for things lost, he found the help he needed.

He studied two sorts of notice, one under "In Memoriam" and the other under "Lost and Found". He preferred the "Lost and Found", liking the idea of posting a reward to indicate you had lost what was important, what was of real value, what you could hardly get along without.

After supper he searched the cabin for his glasses, finding them on the shelf behind the mirror. They were steel-rimmed and hooked behind his ears. Probably they were quite unlike the glasses Mr. Bedford, the railroad surveyor, had worn, lacking, as they did, the long, black ribbon. Still, they served the same purpose, because with their steel rims around his eyes, Nick was disposed for figuring and working with a pencil.

He knocked the end from a prune box and brought it to the table, smoothing its surface with his axe blade until it was white and pleasing to the touch. He took the lantern down, set it by the teapot, and began to carve with his knife on the prune box end, referring in his progress to the want-ad sections of the newspapers, frequently removing his glasses to see better what he was doing. Afterwards, he blacked the letters in with pencil. As the fire in the stove burned low, his fingers grew numb and his pipe perished in his breath, puffed against the lantern.

When he had finished he put on his mackinaw and mitts and beaver cap. Outside, he stood looking for a minute at the failing moon. He hoisted his pack-sack, picked up his axe, and snowshoed eight miles down to the fork in the trail on the way to town. With his axe he cut away the lower branches of a lone standing spruce tree, and blazed flat a section of its trunk. It was a winter blaze above the level of a man's head when the snow had melted into the ground. He nailed the sign there, so placed that it would be seen by anyone coming up or going down the trail.

He stepped back to regard his completed work, stamping his feet, blowing on his fingertips where the frosty steel of the nails had burned. The sign read: "Lost — a white horse named Bedford. The owner offers a reward." At the bottom he carved his own name — "Nick Durban".

During the coming months at least half a dozen men would see the sign and read it. They would be trappers going out with their furs in the spring from the country more to the north, or coming in with supplies in the summer and fall. Each of them would see it twice.

Olaf, the Swede, who was his friend, and who travelled on skis he had hewed and whittled from birch wood, would read it, looking up, stroking his black beard which lay like a young fir tree on his barrelled chest. "By Yimminy, a good horse, a fine horse," he would say, wagging his head, spitting a shaft of brown snoose into the snow. It was Olaf who had taught Bedford to eat bannock. Each visit he made to Nick's cabin he brought a round brown bannock specially baked for the occasion.

And Fred Brewster, the guide and outfitter, would be passing through on his regular hunting party in the fall. He would see the sign, read it aloud to his tourists, who were rich people from the East, and tell them about Bedford. They would know then, all of them, that he was a good horse. If he had not been a good horse, his owner would not have offered a reward.

These men who were neighbours would understand. They

Osprey and nest, Jasper.

Mountain and clouds, Canmore.

Sled dog, Rocky Mountain House.

Ice Sculptor, Winter Cities Festival, Edmonton.

would not go to look for the white horse. They had seen him in his age. They would know that if Nick could not find his horse, then Bedford was where no one would find him again.

Nick returned to his cabin tramping his shadow into the dawn's golden snow. From up toward the High Valley he heard a wolf howl, and then another, and his flesh winced and the pit of his stomach chilled for he knew they had found Bedford.

Later in the month, the thaws having come, he decided to go into town. Formerly he had waited until most of the snow had seeped into the ground so that the white horse could go more easily with him. Now he travelled alone, taking with him on his back his fur catch, the pelts of marten and weasel and those of two silver fox trapped high in the timber.

Approaching the trail forks where he had hung the sign, his pace quickened. By the tree he paused. Someone had been there before him. Brown snoose juice was spattered on the snow. Under the sign was a pattern of ski tracks where Olaf had stopped to read. He had stood there, shaking his head, stroking his beard. Then he had gone down valley, along the other fork of the trail, back to his cabin. It was all there, clear as writing, in the snow. The tracks were three or four days old, their outlines rounded, made before the thaw.

One new set of sharper tracks cut across them, leading up towards the pass. Olaf, apparently, had come this far on his way to town. At the spruce tree he had turned back. Perhaps he had forgotten something at his cabin ten miles down the trail. Then, after a day or two, he had set out again. This time he had not stopped at the sign.

Nick followed on his snowshoes the trail Olaf had broken towards the pass. As he rose above the timber, nearing the summit of the pass, he saw what at first seemed to be a marker Olaf had planted in the snow to mark the trail. Soon he saw that it was too tall, too heavy and that it stood not on the trail, nor beside it, but twenty-five or thirty feet above, close to a wall or rock. Nor was it just one post. It was two, buttressed with stones from a nearby slide. They supported a frame two feet high and three feet wide. Within the frame spruce saplings, peeled of their bark and steamed, had been bent and nailed to form letters.

Nick blinked his eyes, rubbed them, trying to make out the words the letters formed. There were two words, the longer one above the lower. In a minute or two, against the rough,

rock wall behind, they joined, coming alive before him. They spelled "Bedford Pass".

Nick shuffled his shoulders under his pack, stood on one foot and then the other as though the ground beneath his feet were hot. Olaf, who made his own skis, had understood. He had read the sign in the trail forks, had gone back to his cabin to cut and peel and steam and bend and nail the spruce saplings within their frame. He had carried them up to the pass, cut posts from two four-inch jack-pine, and wired the frame to them. Chips and bark were scattered in his many angled ski tracks. His job completed, he had continued on his way into town.

Like the passes in the old country Olaf came from, the pass now had its name. "A pass has its name," Olaf had said. "No one gives one to it." Nick recalled their conversation of long ago.

He went carefully over the letters, one by one, to be sure that the name was correctly spelled. He would have liked the "B" to have been a bit larger. Still, the name would stand there for months, for many years, high on the pass between land and sky. Hunting parties and tourists would see it. People would ask how the pass got its name. Someone would tell them about Bedford, the white horse, the last horse left in the valley from the early days.

Afterwards, the time would come when no one would remember. It would be a name, as the High Valley was a name. Maybe the wind blowing hard from down the valley, or merely a moose or caribou in early September rubbing the velvet from his antlers, would push the posts down. Then the name would sink into the earth and become part of it.

Nick, the first man to cross Bedford Pass, pointed his snowshoes downhill to town and the railroad where Olaf had gone before him. Bedford was now a name. The wolves would not have him. He would outlast flesh and bone and hide and hair. He would endure so long as men climbed rivers to their source and spoke into the wind the pass's name they travelled.

Excerpted from *The Woman Who Got on at Jasper Station and Other Stories*, 1977, reprinted courtesy of Talon Books, Vancouver.

Three skiers, near Fraser Glacier.

Storm on Mount Edith Cavell.

Winter aspens.

Rock ptarmigan, Marmot Basin, Jasper.

Facing the Ramparts, Canadian Alpine Club trip into the Tonquin.

W. J. Phillips, *Mountain Torrent*, 1926, colour woodcut.

# Excerpts from
# *WJP*

by
Jon Whyte

I

Cataract

in chasm

the water falling
shatters
light the light
falling
falls the water
falls    fails
the light fails
the vision
is

still

cataract

    iris

in the ordered
suddenness
of fury's face
and silence
darkness is
ordering

   order
silences

to order
the world
much thatched
much brambled
intertwined
abrim with jams
and tangles
eyes' nettles
the strain
strainer
the mesh
of colours

II
Film forms
on his eye
clear as cataract's
chasm
in chiaroscuro
canyon's water
shattering into
light-scattering
prisms of droplets
his eye forms
informs fills in
a world
to inhabit

   shattering

water shattering
light   wash
of water on shore
of paper
shore of water
is shore of land
paper is shore
world is surface
he faces
surface
is grace
which grace
suffices

   works

a rainbow arc
in the darkness    in clarity
in habit    removing
in serenity    highkey white
inhabited    phenomena
water    flood
water and colour    light
watercolour    whiteness
    the white surrounded
   colour    by colour's
    dappling
    flecks

III

   first
phenomena
and last

waking to morning
waking to mist
soft rain
the ripples
their wakes
of ripples
their wash   wash
of water
the waters of colour
the colours of water

   until

wavering
wavering    wavering
wavering    wavering    wavering

light is like sound spreading its voice
song bright to the ending reverberations

   echoes

the enduring last:

liquidity
the leaf last clings to the bough
bright flag of flame
persistence of autumn

so brief

bright phenomena aflood

living in a flood of still-bright light
days so bright the pain of light
cannot be extinguished

from that light he drew dapplings

the light passes through the shimmers of colour awash
to the retinal fovea (pit of perception: mind's eye)
charged, charges back brightening the colour
as though shone through
               as light shone through sere leaves

        autumn is
        leavetaking

           IV
        Is it built,
        the world?

made about a still contemplative point
        about which
the world moves, or axis; can it be
        made?

        do we move
        our spirit
        the spirit
        moving us

as a hovering bird hesitates
        hoves
        moving unmoving
        over
        the surface
        of lake water

fishhawk, osprey, kingfisher

prey for kingfisher
man fisher, fisherman

        water

is quick as quick as the quickness

        of blood

        the fluid

form of things always changing
to remain the same

better to build from still things
        last leaves
or from the rapid, antic swirlings
        of things?
the world in motion that cries out
        to be held
set to rhythm of its own self

        or

build from the contemplative, the meditative
        home centre
of things where what waves, is moving
in the mind over the water
the fluid spirit over the water?

VI

«The light was steady
but the water!

Rushing at giddying speed
eddying at the brink
churning, rolling, crashing
exploding in spray
not only against rock
but in mid-channel
where currents converged
tumbling, convulsed
boiling in constant ferment . . .»

        each waterfall
        many waterfalls
        all falling a tangle
        torrent of bright-webbed
        water verging
        its many verges

        but fall
        still

«a still camera could never render
such chaotic movement

«the result would be frozen inertia»

        tremble is
        a moving
        standing still

XI

Clarity is
a scoundrel's trick
the secret
carbon simple

        in the complex
        molecules of life

Carbon: coal black, black in the graphite
black as the pencil lead slides on the paper
black as the ash in the spars from the fire
black as silence as absence of noise
black as a blindman's muttered protest
black as a silence void of light

        the stain
        from the lichen
        clings to
        the rock
        after the pioneer
        has deserted
        the surface
        leaving
        traces and tracks
        of varied blacks
        glistening
        in the slick
        gloss of the
        water's path
        a simple black
        tenacity
        that burns
        like life

        the slow
ignition of the leaves: first burst
of unfurling, so large a leaf
cannot within its resinous amber chamber
be refolded. All phenomena irreversible.

The sun cannot withdraw its light.

He chose the natural way, the irreversible,
knowing the place of the place.

XII

We'd watch him. He'd draw in shadows
bold, blue wedges of the steel-shadowing
summer sunlight. And after they were placed
shadows defining shape and substance
he'd fill in the rest with floods of colour
forming the fullness of the range.
And just when we'd say, «Aha!»
(«That is his secret» uttered shortspeech)
he'd change his fashion
draw in the line of crenelates
insert the highlights
dash in the grit and speckled surface
of the rock and, last
place shadows
singing the dark, substantial surface
                    into its relief.
Depth and the tactile reconformed
he'd find an acid contrast in
things as they are.

               Dark in constancy
          the inconstant
          sought solace
          the world appears
          in shifts:
               first veils of mist
          first finery
          the evanescent
          barely plucked
          drift of fine
          translucent
          fabric
          deep blue becoming
          the pale
          suffusing
          blush.

W. J. Phillips, *Vista Lake*, 1932, wood engraving.

# VISTA

Nicholas de Grandmaison, *Many Turning Robes—Blackfoot Indian, ca.* 1930s, drawing.

# Excerpt from
# *BEYOND FORGET,*
# *REDISCOVERING THE*
# *PRAIRIES*

by
Mark Abley

A twining backroad through the Cypress Hills hauled me the following morning into Alberta, the province where my childhood grew like a tame rose. Postcard scenery embraced the car; a sharp whiff of pine freshened its plush interior. The hills contain the highest land in Canada east of the Rocky Mountains, and their lush vegetation escapes the drought of the plains. I was growing accustomed again to the prospect of lakes and evergreen forests when the forest died, the water dried, and the Buffalo Trail began. I had emerged from the bushy topknot of southern Alberta onto its bare, neglected shoulder. A provocative sign reminded the wind and the grass:

NO SERVICE OR
RESIDENCES
NEXT 134 km

A ridge of hills quivered above the southwestern horizon: a blue, far promise: a beckoning.

There were no other drivers. There was no other road. The clouds played hide-and-seek with the sun. A stray fragment of memory fluttered up to consciousness: *Among themselves, American hobos call Canada "Big Lonely."* Framed in my contact lenses, the passing land looked delicate: sagebrush speckled the grasses, smudged with clover and golden bean. . . The frame is an illusion, its perspective a distortion. The land, enclosed by nothing, open to every atrocity of weather, survives far beyond delicacy.

I turned west along a gravel road, leaving the Buffalo Trail to push its unserviced, homeless track into Montana. Over the horizon's lip, the bruise of hills was growing tangible. The gravel and the barbed, unswerving wire had something of the melancholy dignity of a Roman or an Inca road: they offered linear proof that the human race had passed this way. Attempts to farm the region were abandoned early in the century, for even in the fat years after the Armistice, when most people on the prairies were relishing the Years of the Big Wheat, southeastern Alberta lay sick with drought. Its fields have returned to pasture, yet few ranches thrive. That morning I saw as many pairs of

*Opposite:*
Towards the Sweetgrass Hills, from Writing-on-Stone Provincial Park.

antelope as herds of cattle. The rare ponds were already pillows of alkali. And I wondered, as I had in northern Manitoba, whether the advent of white civilization has not left parts of the west emptier than at any time since the last Ice Age.

Antelope, like buffalo, came close to extinction. Their numbers tumbled to fewer than twenty thousand after the ravages of settlement. But thanks to a fast fertility — and the co-operation of ranchers — more than thirty thousand antelope now graze in Canada, and many times that number in the U.S.A. I stopped near the crest of a gradual hill to watch a big male antelope standing indecisively in the middle of the road. The contrast between the animal's stout, muscular body and his needlelike front legs astonished me. He pawed the gravel, nervously shifted, and declined to budge until I drove within a few yards. Then he slipped into the dry ditch and scrambled without elegance under the barbed wire. I would have liked to see him run; pronghorn antelope are the quickest mammal on the continent. Donkeys, however, do not bray to order.

The hill led to, of all things, a village. I had a fine, unhurried view of Manyberries from above: a clump of vehicles and wooden buildings dwarfed by a turquoise elevator of the Alberta Wheat Pool, dwarfed in its turn by a city of fluffy clouds. The clouds outnumbered the houses; so, I eventually saw, did the discarded cars and trucks. "Manyengines" might be a more truthful name.

Drilling rigs from Home Oil and Shell dwindled in the grassy obscurity. A colony of cliff swallows dive-bombed the car. On a paved highway I trundled west beyond Orion, hunting fuel and lunch. The village of Etzikom had neither, nor did it have a Catholic church; one windy night in 1946, the church blew away.

The countryside flattened into rich farmland, some of its vast fields sown to barley, others green with the rising winter wheat. A town called Foremost had a resolute appearance and an empty, sleek Chinese café. The girl who served me was a prodigy of silence: without a word she handed me a menu, took my order, brought me food and tea, and presented a bill. I discovered when I paid that her lips were indeed capable of "Thank you." Starved of verbal stimulation, I was reduced to reading the printed envelope from the People's Republic that encased my jasmine tea bag:

## AROMATIC FLAVOUR! HOMELY REFRESHER!

## GREENISH INFUSION! VALUABLE GIFT!

Refreshed and doubtless homely, I continued westward through the wheat. For the first time in more than eighty springs, the farmers of southern Alberta had refused to plant a crop of sugar beets: a glut of cheap cane from abroad had so depressed the price of beets that every farmer in the region was reverting his fields to grain. As the little towns grew in the windshield — Legend, Skiff, Warner — and shrank in the rearview mirror, their first and last vestige was a grain elevator or two. The standard comparison likens an elevator to a sentinel, but I had decided, after thousands of miles and hundreds of grain elevators, that they resemble giant Monopoly hotels and act like medieval churches — dominating, identifying and justifying the villages in their dusty shade. That day another idea sprang to mind. In their brooding speechlessness, their solemnity above so many withered communities, the elevators are also Canada's towers of silence: its watchers of the prairie dead.

The land was rising. When I headed south, the highway gently breasted the watershed of the Milk River Ridge. Weary of driving, I parked at a glossy motel outside the little town of Milk River. My room contained, among other paraphernalia, four toothpicks wrapped individually in plastic.

I took an instant, irrational dislike to the town. Strolling round it for half an hour, I saw no other person on foot. The town's swank houses stand on streets devoid of sidewalks. What they do have, in grotesque abundance, are garden ornaments. In Milk River, flamingoes, gnomes and Bambis are only the beginning. I found plastic pheasants in front of one splay home, a plastic donkey in front of a second, and a large plastic frog in front of a third. Somewhere between the artificial chickens and the make-believe swans, I passed from disgust to bemusement; by the time I had also marched past a plastic owl and a few sitting ducks, I even felt a grudging respect. Milk River is, to say the least, unique.

Its ornery individuality gives the lie to one of the stranger claims that Heather Robertson made in her brilliant, much-hated book *Grass Roots*. "Prairie towns all look alike," she remarked: "identical grain elevators, identical banks, identical railway stations, a main street that is called Main Street and a road along the tracks called Railway Avenue: when you've seen one, as they say, you've seen 'em all."

Such is the raw form. But the cooking varies dramatically:

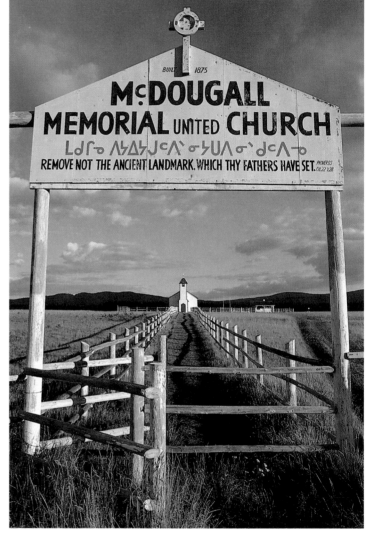

McDougall Church, Morley.

Foxtail barley, east of Markerville, home of Stephán Stephansson, "the poet of the Rocky Mountains" and one of Iceland's major literary figures.

all you need to do is approach the little communities with innocent eyes. Milk River looks no more like Gimli than a village on Galway Bay. Western towns have always differed in their main churches (bulbous Orthodox? trim Protestant? aspiring Catholic?) as well as their settings (a river? a hill? a lake?). Now that most of the towns no longer have active stations, they also differ in the fate of the station house. Some communities have torn it down or allowed it to rot; others have converted it to a museum or a home; in a few, the station houses a business. Even the businesses vary according to the local wealth and traditions. One town's video arcade will be another's Gospel Book Room.

Among the disintegrating villages, too, decay occurs in an assortment of ways and leaves a variety of tracks behind. The process is, unfortunately, common enough to suggest that an unsettled emptiness might be the prairie's destiny. Heather Robertson's central argument — that economic forces, far more than natural ones, are transforming much of the plain into a wasteland — remains sound, however much the inhabitants of prairie cities have loathed her for saying it.

A big lonely sun sliced the horizon far beyond the motel's dining room. My dinner arrived on a platter large enough to hold a turkey. I nibbled for a while and went to bed. Nighttime brought a dense, unexpected rain. Come morning, I drove away with eagerness, basted by a certain fear.

As a child in the early 1960s, I yearned to see the provincial park named Writing-on-Stone. My family lived in Lethbridge, seventy-five miles away, and occasionally my father drove to Waterton Lakes or Calgary or the Crowsnest Pass. But something always forestalled him from Writing-on-Stone: the bad roads, probably, or uncertain weather, or doubts about what he might find there. It remained a country we would forever see "next year." In my mind the place grew mythic. For some reason I thought of it as "Writing-on-the-Wall Park," and I associated it with Belshazzar and messages of ancient doom. Even in childhood, I guess, my imagination veered towards apocalypse.

We moved to Saskatoon when I was twelve, and Writing-on-Stone became a green triangle on a disused map. I was growing up; I had other discoveries to make. "You'll study law," I was instructed, or "You'll major in political science," or "You'll go through graduate school." I raised an inward eyebrow, faithful to my own suspicions, although they were yet too molten to

Looking over the Old Man River Valley to the Porcupine Hills.

cohere into hard plans. Lecture rooms and courtrooms and committee rooms — the smoky realm of offices and hard-bitten backs — held small appeal for me. I felt that to be a creator of messages, a teller of tales, would prove an honourable calling. An image of desire and loss flickered at the back of my mind. But I quit the prairies without finishing the dream.

Now that I was back in Alberta, the idea of the park made me strangely nervous. How could it match my yearning? I was nostalgic, perhaps, for the illusions of childhood, when the future was radiant with power and unlimited choice.

The future had come. I was driving through it on a paved, slippery road. The morning wind churned up puddles under a morose sky. "A miracle rain," the waitress had told me gladly in the pancake-scented motel, "the only thing that could stop the grasshoppers!" My car scudded past the wet fields of wheat. Listening to the Voice of Southern Alberta, I learned that the poisonous fogs against grasshoppers and cutworms were murdering the region's honey. A farmer north of Milk River had lost six million bees in a cloud. I was contemplating that glum total when the road switched to gravel and pulled me into the park.

Writing-on-Stone Park is small and dramatic. It exists where nature, as though bored at last with the great scraped mat of prairie, has humped herself to form cones, pinnacles and fallen arches: a serpentine Carnival slithering through a Lenten plain. Outcrops of sandstone, twisted by wind and water into bulging hoodoos, flanked the car. Capped by its hard deposits of ironstone, the sandstone has eroded into shapes that defy probability. I drove cautiously down through a city of tawny sculptures to the bushy valley of the Milk.

Some of the sandstone cliffs, scoured by centuries of blown dust, made an ideal screen on which to record a skirmish, a rite of passage, a flight of spirit. Usually the recorders carved or scratched their tale; occasionally they would paint it in ochre. The visual language of the messages was familiar to the many Indian bands — Shoshoni, Blackfoot, Sioux, Plains Cree and others — who roamed the prairies for food and took shelter among the Milk's cottonwoods and willows. The valley was no one's property; its gifts were gifts for all. It became a sacred place.

But the messages are growing more and more secret. Rubbed by cattle, defaced by vandals, eaten by rough weather and alkali salts from within, the images are approaching their final silence. "Here, take this map," a warden said that morning, handing

me a crowded chart of stylized horses, tipis and men at war. He told me where to look for the battle in a virgin forest of stone. I climbed out of the groves and riverside glades, and strolled for twenty minutes across a high scrap of plain. A muscular wind began to clear the sky; the sun appeared in force. Scarlet mallow, blue flax and the first wild roses of summer shone in the grass. Droplets of the night's rain still clung onto stalks and petals. Below them, a good path fell to the outcrops.

It took me a long time to reach the battle scene, for I was dazzled by the grace of the park. It compressed so many landscapes into so little space. Its birds, refreshed by rain and sun, were exuberant: rock wrens dappled the cliffs; towhees darted in the thickets; a patient heron fished from a sandbank at the river's curling edge. I grew bored waiting by a patch of musineon — the clustered flowers resembled lemon-coloured broccoli — for a snoozing doe to budge. She was lying, catlike, on a ledge beside the path, her chin resting on her outspread forelegs; catlike, she looked annoyed when I gave up waiting and clumped down the trail.

I found the battle scene and felt a fool. The chart disclosed what I might have been able to see: a complicated fight involving rifles, arrows, spears and a big axe. Horsemen were attacking a ring of tipis. The defence was strenuous, the outcome unsure. My eyes might have picked out dozens of warriors from the early nineteenth century as they struggled for glory and stolen horses. But all I could discern was a faint scattering of grooves and crosses on a pock-marked cliff. Does every vision quest collapse into a question of visibility?

Depressed, I clambered to a viewpoint and gazed across the river. And there, beckoning over a few grazed miles, were the blue-green buttes I had seen from the far-off Buffalo Trail. To a plains Indian, these Sweetgrass Hills and the Milk's sinuous valley form part of the same land. In my terms, unfortunately, the hills lie on private property just south of the 49th Parallel. I still imagined that somewhere on their firred, lithe slopes a message might await me. But if childhood means a longing for adult power, adulthood means an acceptance of power's borders. The Sweetgrass Hills rise beyond my personal territory. I may dream of them, and nothing more.

In the hills' shadow, the North-West Mounted Police created one of its most isolated posts. The policemen who lived there fought fires, guarded horses and relieved a famine or two; most of all, they were border patrolmen charged with keeping

American cattle and liquor out of Canada. The latter task proved the harder. When the Canadian northwest was dry, smugglers hauled alcohol across the Medicine Line disguised in casks of flour and cartons of eggs, or even in the underwear of "pregnant" women who enjoyed miscarriages a mile out of Montana. Depression was common for the lonesome mounties, and temptation close at hand: in 1892, five of the six constables at Writing-on-Stone deserted to the wet U.S.A.

By 1918, when the outpost closed, the boundary was mostly fenced and the ranchland mostly docile. The annual Writing-on-Stone Stampede — still held in a wooden corral at the park's edge — had become a tradition. The first stampede, which celebrated the British king's birthday in 1910, included a race between a dog and a horse.

The dog won. I could imagine all that history; it was recorded in my own tongue. But with the other, foreign stories — the messages on stone — I needed help. I retreated to the warden's office and asked to see a fragment of the Archaeological Preserve in Eileen Hassett's company.

Eileen had a serious, efficient air; her directness of manner and the calmness of her voice bespoke a practical competence. But her warden's uniform camouflaged a romantic, even obsessive devotion to Writing-on-Stone. Her descriptions of the hoodoos under a tuque of snow or the moonstruck Milk on a summer night's canoe trip invested her eyes with love.

She drove a van into the preserve, which lies out of bounds for unescorted visitors, and we scrambled down a sharp hill to a pack of outcrops. Shrubs and slender trees stretched below the path to the water. By now the jagged, rumpled rocks seemed as natural to me as a field or a forest. The common adjective "weird" turns to a lie after the second glance.

"What do you see there?"

I squinted at some carved lines. They suggested a freehand drawing of a fish.

"No idea."

"Well, it's a fish," Eileen said. She pointed out adjacent images in the panel: a horse with a long lifeline, two men with pointed shoulders, and an odd humanoid figure with a semicircular head. The more she explained, the more I saw.

"So what could this be?" I asked.

In my enthusiasm I had pressed two fingers against the stone.

"Don't touch it!" Eileen said at once. "Please! — I'm not sure about that image. A man praying to the spirits, maybe?"

We moved slowly on, past a headless man and a phallic man

and a buffalo. In one superb panel, a child was born beside a battle. Its labouring mother stretched an arm backwards to the shielded warriors. Form was inseparable from content, gesture from emotion. The image's force was tense and raw.

"Will you look at this?"

I thought that Eileen must be pointing to a rare carving at ground level. But when I looked, I saw a cottontail rabbit cowering under a bush, trapped between four legs and a rock. Its ears had been pushed into the lustrous auburn fur of its back in an effort to hide. Above the rabbit stood a carving of a bugling elk. We stayed there talking for a few minutes, and the rabbit relaxed enough to resume a watchful nibbling.

It's like learning a foreign language," Eileen said. "You have to work at it, and ask a lot of questions, and try not to get frustrated. Sooner or later, it all starts to make sense."

Yet the erosion and defacement are enough to ensure that the full story will never be known. Even to Eileen's eyes, the images retain a quality of mystery. Because of their inscrutable power, the carvings have attracted explanations far more contorted than the hoodoos. Back in 1952 Henriette Mertz suggested that the stones were inscribed by Chinese explorers in the twenty-third century B.C. Later dreamers have proposed that the lines and grooves are specimens of Ogham — a system of writing developed by the ancient Celts. Or if the Ogham theory fails to hold, perhaps the carvings could be Viking runes?

Certainly there is much about the ancient world that escapes understanding. Writing-on-Stone tantalizes: one of its hoodoos contains a carving of the three-legged wheel of life, a symbol that adorns Greek coins from Sicily and the heraldic emblem of the Isle of Man. But to my mind, the desire to prove an exotic influence at Writing-on-Stone — and other Indian sites across the continent — has a malign undertone. Whether they aim to show the range of Celtic or Norse exploration, the pervasiveness of Chinese or Polynesian culture, many writers erode the accomplishments of native people. They suggest that the art of the Indians depended on inspiration from beyond. Their dogged labours remind me of the discredited essays of Englishmen who denied that a performer from a small town, never blessed by a degree or a pedigree, could have composed *The Tempest* or *King Lear*. For decades scholars tried to prove that Sir Francis Bacon, or the Earl of Southampton, or some other appropriate gentleman had used the pen name "Shakespeare." Yet in truth, just as a provincial actor wrote *Lear*,

Shaftsbury Ferry across the Peace.

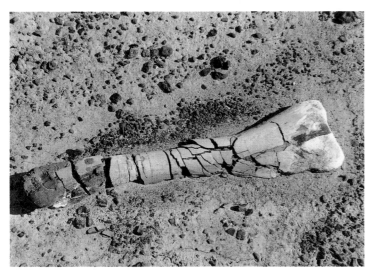
75,000,000 year old dinosaur bone, Badlands of the Red Deer River.

so too did the plains Indians create the visual grammar and the graphic vocabulary of Writing-on-Stone.

"Do Indians ever come to the park?" I asked.

"Sure," Eileen said. "Some of them still leave a gift for the spirits."

"What kind of gift?"

"A wad of tobacco. Or a string of beads."

Halfway up a cottonwood sapling near the river, a porcupine had come to rest. The trunk looked too flimsy to support its fat, yellow-quilled body.

"I guess they don't tell you everything they know."

She nodded. "That's the problem. If it *is* a problem. One time I was showing the images to some people from the Peigan reserve, and an old woman suddenly turned away and walked down the trail till she was out of sight. We caught up with her when we moved on. I asked her why, and she finally told me: it was forbidden for her to look at that particular scene."

"You don't know why it was forbidden?"

"I could make a guess. That's all."

The images erode to silence yet, in some minds, the spirit remains. The powers be. They inscribe their ancient messages on our paper skins or our stone hearts in ways that we perhaps fail to recognize, let alone control. To the Indian who travelled through the Milk River valley, the rocks held out a vision of experience and a promise in the jaws of time. The rocks were oracles where a wanderer might glimpse, like a dream passing across the face of stone, the pattern written for his life.

"They believe," Eileen said, "that to even look at some of the images can be dangerous. The story goes that a hunter once camped here in a certain place alone. He disregarded all the warnings of the medicine men. And the next morning he was found stumbling across the prairie — blind."

I left the park. Beyond its sweet domain, the blue remembered hills stretched out like a resting body. Exhilaration and astonishment had given way in me to something approaching joy. Not to have made the pilgrimage would have been dangerous: a denial of my childhood; a rejection of its incomplete dream. The English name of the park had worked its power but I decided, in the end, that the Blackfoot word *aysin'eep* was more eloquent and more exact. Aysin'eep means "is being written."

East of Trochu.

# Excerpt from
## *WOLF WILLOW*

by
Wallace Stegner

The geologist who surveyed southern Saskatchewan in the 1870's called it one of the most desolate and forbidding regions on earth. I can remember plenty of times when it seemed so to me and my family. Yet as I poke the car tentatively eastward into it from Medicine Hat, returning to my childhood through a green June, I look for desolation and can find none.

The plain spreads southward below the Trans-Canada Highway, an ocean of wind-troubled grass and grain. It has its remembered textures: winter wheat heavily headed, scoured and shadowed as if schools of fish move in it; spring wheat with its young seed-rows as precise as combings in a boy's wet hair; gray-brown summer fallow with the weeds disked under; and grass, the marvelous curly prairie wool tight to the earth's skin, straining the wind as the wheat does, but in its own way, secretly.

Prairie wool blue-green, spring wheat bright as new lawn, winter wheat gray-green at rest and slaty when the wind flaws it, roadside primroses as shy as prairie flowers are supposed to be, and as gentle to the eye as when in my boyhood we used to call them wild tulips, and by their coming date the beginning of summer.

On that monotonous surface with its occasional ship-like farm, its atolls of shelter-belt trees, its level ring of horizon, there is little to interrupt the eye. Roads run straight between parallel lines of fence until they intersect the circle of the horizon. It is a landscape of circles, radii, perspective exercises — a country of geometry.

Across its empty miles pours the pushing and shouldering wind, a thing you tighten into as a trout tightens into fast water. It is a grassy, clean, exciting wind, with the smell of distance in it, and in its search for whatever it is looking for it turns over every wheat blade and head, every pale primrose, even the ground-hugging grass. It blows yellow-headed blackbirds and hawks and prairie sparrows around the air and ruffles the short tails of meadowlarks on fence posts. In collaboration with the light, it makes lovely and changeful what might otherwise be characterless.

It is a long way for characterless; "overpowering" would be a better word. For over the segmented circle of earth is domed the biggest sky anywhere, which on days like this sheds down on range and wheat and summer fallow a light to set a painter wild, a light pure, glareless, and transparent. The horizon a dozen miles away is as clean a line as the nearest fence. There is no haze, neither the woolly gray of humid countries nor the blue atmosphere of the mountain West. Across the immense sky move navies of cumuli, fair-weather clouds, their bottoms as even as if they had scraped themselves flat against the flat earth.

The drama of this landscape is in the sky, pouring with light and always moving. The earth is passive. And yet the beauty I am struck by, both as present fact and as revived memory, is a fusion: this sky would not be so spectacular without this earth to change and flow and darken under it. And whatever the sky may do, however the earth is shaken or darkened, the Euclidean perfection abides. The very scale, the hugeness of simple forms, emphasizes stability. It is not hills and mountains which we should call eternal. Nature abhors an elevation as much as it abhors a vacuum; a hill is no sooner elevated than the forces of erosion begin tearing it down. These prairies are quiescent, close to static; looked at for any length of time, they begin to impose their awful perfection on the observer's mind. Eternity is a peneplain.

In a wet spring such as this, there is almost as much sky on the ground as in the air. The country is dotted with sloughs, every depression is full of water, the roadside ditches are canals. Grass and wheat grow to the water's edge and under it; they seem to grow right under the edges of the sky. In deep sloughs tules have rooted, and every such pond is dignified with mating mallards and the dark little automata that glide after them as if on strings.

The nesting mallards move in my memory, too, pulling after them shadowy, long-forgotten images. The picture of a drake standing on his head with his curly tailfeathers sticking up from a sheet of wind-flawed slough is tangled in my remembering senses with the feel of the grassy edge under my bare feet, the smell of mud, the push of the traveler wind, the weight of the sun, the look of the sky with its level-floored clouds made for the penetration of miraculous Beanstalks.

Desolate? Forbidding? There was never a country that in its good moments was more beautiful. Even in drouth or dust storm or blizzard it is the reverse of monotonous, once you have submitted to it with all the senses. You don't get out of the wind, but learn to lean and squint against it. You don't escape sky and sun, but wear them in your eyeballs and on your back. You become acutely aware of yourself. The world is very large, the sky even larger, and you are very small. But also the world is flat, empty, nearly abstract, and in its flatness you are a challenging upright thing, as sudden as an exclamation mark, as enigmatic as a question mark.

It is a country to breed mystical people, egocentric people, perhaps poetic people. But not humble ones. At noon the total sun pours on your single head; at sunrise or sunset you throw a shadow a hundred yards long. It was not prairie dwellers who invented the indifferent universe or impotent man. Puny you may feel there, and vulnerable, but not unnoticed. This is a land to mark the sparrow's fall.

Illingworth Kerr, *Magpies, Winter Sun*, n.d., linocut.

# ANCIENT TIMES

Don McVeigh, *La Baie*, 1986, watercolour.

Hoodoos, Drumheller.

# Excerpt from
# *BADLANDS*

by
Robert Kroetsch

*Anna Dawe*

*Just as my name was determined in that season eleven years before I was born, so were my character, my fate. For in that summer of his glory my father became not only what he had always implicitly been, but what he explicitly wanted to be. After that he was a man without a history, for in that season he became the man that twenty-six more seasons, in the bonebeds of the world, would only confirm. Failure might have ruined him back into history; but failure was never to be his good fortune. It is true that success never made him wealthy. But my mother's sense of guilt, or pride, or perhaps her need to keep him in the field, provided him with the means to live beyond his income. And beyond us as well.*

*It was in my fate to dream a father, in my character to wait. And I waited for ten years after his death, as if he must bring himself back from his own bonebed.*

*Surely, yes, I worked at the waiting; as he had worked at his starting out. I studied the documents. I read of the bitter feuds of Marsh and Cope, those first great collectors of dinosaur bones; and from that lesson I learned mostly that my father had been born one generation too late. But he was not to be deterred by a mere error in chronology. My mother and I read his field notes, and then I read them alone. And we — I — read of his ventures into deserts and jungles, into Africa and Texas and Patagonia, into the Arctic islands. I read of his brave and absurd and (needless to say) successful expeditions into Mongolia — in search of dinosaur eggs. But while he went on, annually if not endlessly, collecting evidence of Cretaceous and then Jurassic and then Triassic life; while he persisted as if he must one happy morning get back to the source itself, the root moment when the glory of reptiles, destined to dominate the world magnificently for one hundred million years, was focussed in one bony creature, one Adam-seed burrowing in the green slime —*

*But I was left always with the mystery of his own first season. For in his summer of 1916, in the Badlands of the Red Deer River, discovering the Mesozoic era, with all of Europe filling its earth with the bones of its own young — he removed himself from time.*

*Whatever the desperate reason that had taken him into that far place, he came back delivered of most of the impulses we like to think of as human. He could survive any weather, any diet, any deprivation. And that was necessary to a man whose back bore on it a hump larger than any of us could see. But*

*somewhere in the course of that first journey that was his own — somewhere, somehow, he shook himself free of any need to share even his sufferings with another human being. His field notes, after that summer, were less and less concerned with his crew, his dangers, his days of futile prospecting, his moments of discovery, his weariness, his ambitions, his frustrations. They became scientific descriptions of the size and location of bones, of the composition of the matrix, of the methods of extraction and preservation. . .*

*And I had to visit those badlands where his success began. Because, there, in that beautiful and nightmare season — he ceased to dare to love.*

*26. Deadlodge Canyon at Last*

Dawe writing: *Wednesday, July 5. Into Oldman formation. Moved downriver at dawn. Hot by 9 a.m. Herons wading in the shallows. A mule deer watching from a cliff. The landscape dusty and dry and brown beyond the green at the river's edge. Making shore-camp now, below the mouth of Little Sandhill Creek. Eight miles from rimrock to farthest rimrock, the canyon itself extending downriver, how many miles I won't guess.* Web, as we landed, looking up at the endless buttes coulees: "Where did you say you dropped that needle?"

"Where's the pickaxe?" Tune said.

"Woops," Web said. "Knew we forgot something."

They were setting up a second tent, for the cook; Grizzly insisted that the cook's tent be well up on dry land, on the sagebrush flat above the cutbank, with cottonwoods and poplars nearby, a huge patch of thorny buffalo berries outside the tent flaps. They would leave the main tent on the boat, where they might sleep at night in a breeze, free from mosquitoes and the heat.

"What should I do?" Tune said. "Can't drive a stake in this ground."

*I could have hit Web with an axe. But he's right. Now that we're here: where do I begin —*

And Dawe, then, telling his crew: "Unload the lumber and the plaster of paris. Get a decent table built. Lay in a supply of firewood for Grizzly." And Dawe himself bent over his open steamer trunk, locating a specimen bag, a small pick, a brush, a compass. Dawe striking out: alone, hurrying, he walked out across the flat, finding a path through the sagebrush, the blue-grey hairs of the sage, the twisted, upthrust branches blurring his figure, only his strange back, his black hat, clearly in motion.

Red Deer River, near Rumsey.

White tail deer.

He turned off the flat, away from the river and up onto a ridge, went over and down, into a dry creek bed where not the slightest breeze stirred; and moving up the wall of a butte he found no relief, the sun glaring off the layered clay, off the rust-colored ironstone, the grey bentonite.

He was breathing too hard and he sat down on a boulder to rest; he must learn to move more slowly in the heat. Must. Wrong time to commence. Dizzy from hunger and heat and thirst. Precipitous. High noon the wrong time.

He started back towards the boat — towards camp: Grizzly's stove should be ashore, the fire lit. Time for dinner. Eat a square meal. Look for that canteen and down to the river and fill it. Dehydration can kill a man. After too damned much water for too long.

He almost fell into a deserted quarry.

The hole in the side of the butte had been hacked out, gouged out, by men working in this heat. Dawe thinking, hazily, bitterly: Brown and his five skilled assistants. Sternberg and his three sons and their trained crew. Dawe, down over the crest of the butte, staring into the empty niche. Already the sudden, harsh rains of three seasons, four seasons, had softened the broken edges of clay. But the hole was there, gaping, huge, reminding Dawe that his was only the latest, not the first, expedition. And if nothing new, nothing of importance was to be found, then not only the latest but the last. Skunked. The booby prize.

He walked into camp and found Tune and Web wrestling the stove up the cutbank. Dawe trying the cook's tent and finding it stuffy hot, going down to the river, back to the flatboat from which he had thought himself freed. Dawe, pretending he was busy, pretending he wasn't afraid: *The hole is empty. Redundant. Be careful of the sun. Redundant. A hunchback will, easily, if exerting himself beyond the natural, suffer from anoxia.* He looked at what he had written. He felt safer. *Redundant*, he dared to add.

Web and Tune, sweating, came up the gang-plank to begin to unload the lumber, the wood for the packing boxes. Dawe, putting away his stub of pencil:

"Where did Grizzly get to?"

Tune, mopping his forehead with the tail of his shirt. "Went somewhere with a fishing pole."

Web groaned aloud. "Can't be another god-damned goldeye in this river. I absolutely refuse to choke on, spit out or swallow another fishbone."

Grizzly, small, silent, hurrying, came out of the cottonwoods that bordered the water; he was carrying his fishing rod and three goldeyes.

Badlands, Dinosaur Provincial Park.

### 27. Looking for Fossils

Next morning Dawe took Tune and Web with him into the coulees, showed Tune, showed Web again, how to recognize a fossil if there chanced to be a fossil to be recognized. Without a fragment to look at he tried to tell them of creatures no one had ever seen, explained how to watch for the brown concretion that wasn't quite brown, the texture that wasn't merely rock, the shape that couldn't be expected to have been bone but wasn't quite anything else. And on the morning of the day after that day he elaborated further, unwilling to believe they had learned their lesson, believing they had not learned, for if they had they would not have failed so miserably as had he; he who could (blindfolded, he explained to Tune) without fail recognize a gastrolith or a horn cone in the rubble at the base of a cliff, a vertebra in a concretion in a sandstone outcrop. And that day, too, they learned again how to move slowly, the thermometer in the tent's shade reading 105 degrees by 2 p.m., how to make a canteen of water last, how not to drink too much when they returned to camp and fell down flat on the bank and dipped their faces into the river. And on the evening of that (third) day Dawe wrote something on page 39, Book A, of his field notes for 1916, then tore off the bottom half of the page and, presumably, destroyed it: Dawe, at last, come to doubt.

### 28. House of Bone

Smoke, as they commenced the fourth day of their prospecting, billowed down into and filled the long canyon. Somewhere to the west a prairie fire burned unchecked, the drifting clouds of smoke blurring the buttes with a veil that in its diffusion of light produced a blue-grey glare. The three men, out prospecting, kept their eyes to the ground, learned quickly they could lose each other from sight, learned quickly to listen. And it was Dawe's intense listening, not his sight, that led him to his first discovery.

He was little more than a mile below camp, returning from the day's vain search, when he heard a voice that he took to be Tune's. The voice lifted into song. He was so exhausted he had passed it by, had passed by the singing, before he understood it was in a language that neither he nor Tune might know.

Dawe turned off the sagebrush flat, turned back, entered a clump of old cottonwoods.

The singing resumed.

Weather-vane.

He took another thirty paces, forty paces, broke through the circle of trees and into a dry gulch.

The heap of dinosaur bones at first appeared to him to be just that: he recognized at a glance the fragments of ribs and vertebrae, of the shells of turtles, of skulls, of long bones. He believed for a moment he was losing his mind, in the aimless light, was fantasying the bones he had not been able to find in four days of searching. Without a pause he began to walk in a circle around the heaped and apparently singing bones, vaguely aware as he did so that the fragments were arranged in some sort of pattern.

Then, on the river side, he came to the opening, two five-foot femurs, crossed against each other, tied to make an inverted vee.

He did not have to step inside.

Anna Yellowbird came to the low doorway, stooped from her dugout, her cabin of bones, her fossil tipi.

"Come in," she said.

She was as tall as the silent man who confronted her. It was his speechlessness, his absolute loss for words, that made him obey. He stooped after her into the tipi, straightened in the small and conical room. Saw, in looking about him in the subdued light, an axe that was from his boat, a blanket that was from his boat, a tarpaulin from his boat, food from his boat.

He might have reached up, had he been able, might have brought the bones crashing down upon their heads. And even as he confronted the futility of that proposal, he recognized that the girl, the child, the woman, had had help in building her strange house: from one or more or all of the men who were supposedly helping him seek these rare and precious specimens.

Dawe did not speak. It was the sheer domesticity of the scene that broke him away and back to the doorway. It was not the heaped and mysterious bones themselves, not the grotesque doorway of the joined thighbones of a hadrosaur nor the stacked and interlocked fragments of fish and turtles and petrified wood; not the broken and fragmented limbs and hips, the bony shields, the huge pelvic bones, the teeth, the jaws, but the fire in the middle of the small room, the pot by the fire, the knife and fork by the pot.

Soon," the woman said, Anna Yellowbird said, "we will find them."

Dawe stepped out of the tipi, out into the failing day, turned, found the path into the crooked trees and through them, stumbled out onto the sagebrush flat, followed what to him looked like a path, a new, worn path through the sagebrush and the buffalo-berry bushes.

Barbara Leighton [Barleigh], *Range Gossip*, n.d., woodcut. A "Barleigh" is a woodcut by Barbara Leighton, which has been taken from a painting by her husband, A. C. Leighton.

# THE WRITERS

**Mark Abley** was born in Leamington Spa, England, but grew up in Lethbridge and Saskatoon. He was a regular contributor to *Maclean's* and *Saturday Night* before writing *Beyond Forget: Discovering the Prairies* in 1986.

☆

**R. Ross Annett** was a principal in Consort when "It's Gotta Rain Sometime" was accepted by the *Saturday Evening Post* in 1938. It was the first of 72 short stories that won him fame in Canada and the United States as a regular contributor to the *Post*, with a weekly circulation of six million copies. He is now retired and living in Edmonton.

☆

**Edmund Kemper Broadus** (1876-1936) was born in Alexandria, Virginia. Drawn from Harvard to the University of Alberta by Henry Marshall Tory in 1908, Broadus went on to have a profound impact on generations of students as a Professor of English. *Saturday and Sunday* was a collection of essays written for the *Atlantic Monthly*, the *London Mercury* and *University Magazine*

☆

**Annora Brown** (1899-1987) was born in Fort Macleod. As a well known painter of the wild flowers of the West, she wrote and illustrated the classic on prairie flora, *Old Man's Garden*. Her autobiography *Sketches of Life* is a fascinating account of the career of an Alberta artist.

☆

**Lovat Dickson** (1902-1987) was born in Australia and lived in South Africa and England before coming to Canada at the age of 15. He was a student of E.K. Broadus at the University of Alberta before embarking on a remarkable career as a writer, editor, and publisher. His many books include *Wilderness Man: The Story of Grey Owl, The Ante-Room,* and *House of Words*. He founded his own publishing house and later became a director of Macmillan of London.

☆

**Bob Edwards** (1864-1922) was born in Edinburgh and emigrated to Western Canada in 1894. He was intermittently the editor of the Calgary *Eye Opener* between 1902 to 1922. Lampooning a wide range of Alberta high society, especially political figures, he was the target of more than his share of legal actions. He won election to the Provincial Legislature as an independent in 1921, but was only able to attend one sitting before his untimely death.

☆

**Caterina Edwards** was born in Wellingborough, England but spent much of her youth in Calgary. She now teaches Canadian literature in Edmonton. Her short studies have been published in *Dandelion, Branching Out,* and the *Journal of Canadian Fiction* and in various anthologies. In 1982 she published her first novel, *The Lion's Mouth.*

☆

**Joy Kogawa** was born in Vancouver. A Japanese Canadian, she witnessed the internment and persecution of her people during the Second World War. She has worked as a school teacher and is widely published as a poet. *Obasan*, her first novel, won the 1982 Canadian Authors' Association Book of the Year Award.

☆

**Myrna Kostash** was born and raised in Edmonton. She is a widely published free-lance journalist whose work has appeared in *Saturday Night, Maclean's,* and *Chatelaine.* Her books include *All of Baba's Children*, a study of Ukrainian-Canadian ethnicity, and *A Long Way From Home*, a memory of the political movements of the 1960s.

☆

**Henry Kreisel** was born in Vienna. He came to Canada in 1940, studied at the University of Toronto, then came west to write and teach at the University of Alberta, where he became one of the first people to bring the experience of the immigrant to modern Canadian literature. He has published two novels — *The Rich Man* (1948) and *The Betrayal* (1964) — and his short stories have recently been collected in the book, *The Almost Meeting* (1981).

☆

**Robert Kroetsch**. Born in Heisler and a graduate of the University of Alberta, Kroetsch has written extensively about the west in *Alberta, But We Are Exiles, The Wards of My Roaring, Gone Indian, Badlands*, and *Studhorse Man*, for which he won the Governor General's Award for fiction in 1969.

☆

**W. O. Mitchell**. The author of *Who Has Seen the Wind*, one of the best loved of Canadian novels, and *Jake and the Kid*, Mitchell has recently published *How I Spent My Summer Holidays*, in addition to *The Vanishing Point*. He was born in Weyburn, Saskatchewan. In 1973 he received the Order of Canada.

☆

**Howard O'Hagan** was born in Lethbridge and was one of the first native-born Albertans to make a mark on Canadian literature. He wrote two novels, *Tay John* and *The School-Marm Tree*, and two selections of short stories, *Wilderness Man* and *The Woman who got on at Jasper Station and Other Stories*. Many considered him the quintessential mountain man whose fiction celebrates the Canadian Wilderness and the people who explored it.

☆

**Judy Schultz** is a professional eater. Her special brand of foodwriting has entertained readers for the past ten years, first in the pages of *Western Living* magazine, then in *The Edmonton Journal*, where she became food editor in 1982. As the restaurant critic of record in Alberta's capital city, she is tough but fair. Her popular column, Dining Out, has made the Sunday edition of the *Journal* required reading for thousands of fans. Her first book, *Dining Out in Edmonton*, appeared in 1983, her second *Nibbles and Feasts* was published in 1986.

☆

**Allan Shute**. When he is not tracking down litterbugs or capturing Riverdale history, Allan Shute acts as publisher at Tree Frog Press, Western Canada's foremost specialist in children's literature, established in 1971. A native Edmontonian, Shute was born April 19, 1945, and was educated locally. He graduated from the University of Alberta in 1969 with an M.A. in English Literature by writing "a fairy tale of the absurd" as his thesis requirement.

☆

Wallace Stegner was born in Iowa and spent his youth in many areas of the United States and the Canadian Northwest. *Wolf Willow* is at once a history, a story, and a memory of the last plains frontier he encountered as a boy in southwestern Saskatchewan. His many novels include *The Spectator Bird*, which won the National Book Award, and *Angle of Repose* which won a Pulitzer Prize.

☆

Merna Summers was born in Mannville. She has worked as a writer for the *Edmonton Journal* and has written for television and radio. Her story "Threshing Time" won the Katherine Anne Porter Prize in 1979.

☆

Lewis Gwynne Thomas is a professor/emeritus of Canadian History at the University of Alberta. His many articles and two books, *Ranchers' Legacy* and *The Liberal Party in Canada* have been major contributions to the history of the west. He is an avid gardener.

Jon Whyte was born in Banff where he developed a poet's fascination with the myths, characters, and stories of the Canadian Rockies. Three collections of his work, *The Fells of Brightness, Homage, Henry Kelsey*, and *Gallimaufry*, have been published to wide critical acclaim. He is currently curator of the Heritage collection of the Whyte Museum of the Canadian Rockies in Banff.

☆

Rudy Wiebe was born in Saskatchewan and now lives in Edmonton. He teaches Canadian literature and creative writing at the University of Alberta. His novels include *Peace Shall Destroy Many, The Mad Trapper, My Lovely Enemy*, and *The Temptations of Big Bear* which won the Governor General's Award for fiction.

# THE ARTISTS

James Agrell-Smith (b.1913). Agrell-Smith was born in Stettler, Alberta. He painted and drew in his early years but has largely worked in engraving and woodblock printmaking for nearly forty years. He is self-taught and believes that an artist should strive to perfect his or her craft. His intense, direct prints describe poetically the actions and objects of everyday life, usually the rural life of which he is so fond.

☆

Elliott Chapell Barnes (1866-1938). Barnes was an American outdoorsman who immigrated to southern Alberta in 1905 with his family to ranch on the Kootenay Plains. He also became a wilderness packer, guide, and photographer of the Banff area. He was a romantic whose vision of the Canadian wilderness was a unique combination of ruggedness and gentility.

☆

Maxwell Bates (1906-1980). An architect and a painter, Bates painted the prairie landscape with an impressive strength of line and an essential understanding of the place, freely and spontaneously done. Bates was born in Calgary and was primarily a figurative painter who produced relatively few landscapes. Bates was greatly influenced by French modernism, studied art in England and New York and eventually gave up architecture completely in 1961.

☆

Annora Brown (1899-1987). Brown grew up in the prairie town of Fort Macleod where she was born. She studied at the Ontario College of Art, and taught art in Alberta for many years. She was primarily a painter of wild flowers. Her love of the natural beauty of the prairie and of local Indian lore culminated in perhaps her best known work, *Old Man's Garden*, which she illustrated with linocuts of the flowers and animals of the Old Man River area.

Ihor Dmytruk (b.1938). Ukrainian-born, Dmytruk's family emigrated to Canada in 1949. His art studies were at the University of Alberta and the Vancouver School of Art. He has taught at the University of Alberta Faculty of Extension since 1964. Dmytruk has worked in many media: woodcut, watercolour, photography, drawing, and acrylic. In the early 1970s his meticulous studies of geometric, man-made urban forms received critical attention. In recent years he has abstracted the landscape in miniature and large-scale acrylic paintings.

☆

H.G. Glyde (b.1906). Glyde was born and studied art in England. He came to the Canadian prairies in the 1930s and has been an influential force through his thirty years as an art educator and painter. He was at various times head of the art departments of the University of Alberta, the Provincial Institute of Technology and Art in Calgary, and the Banff School of Fine Arts. His major works are oils and murals that portray urban and rural prairie life in a realistic yet allegorical style.

☆

Nicholas de Grandmaison (1892-1978). De Grandmaison was born in Moscow of French descent. He studied art there and in London and immigrated to Canada in 1923, eventually settling in Alberta. He painted landscapes and the cowboy, but it is for his sensitive portraits of North American Indians that he is best known.

☆

Byron Harmon (1876-1942). Harmon was born in Tacoma, Washington, and from his early childhood, was interested in photography. Later he worked as a travelling portrait photographer. His travels ended when he arrived in the Rockies and he settled permanently in Banff around 1900, establishing himself as a photographer and businessman. He has left a huge legacy of photographs of the Rockies as they were before extensive development forever removed those pristine days from our view.

**Carole Harmon.** Without Carole Harmon's effort, the photo legacy of her grandfather may not have been preserved and brought to the public attention. She has organized a book and a major North American exhibition of his work as well as being a well-known photographer in her own right.

☆

**Alex Janvier** (b.1935). Janvier was born in Cold Lake, Alberta, and studied at the Alberta College of Art in Calgary. His flowing, colourful, almost calligraphic prints and gouaches have been described as bridges between Indian and European art. Perhaps the bridge will expand to the East, for in 1985 he was one of three visual artists selected by the Canada Council to represent Canada on a three-week cultural exchange with China, an experience that has been the basis of much recent work.

☆

**Illingworth Kerr** (b.1905). As a young boy in his native Saskatchewan, Kerr first became interested in drawing the land and animals around him. He eventually studied with members of the Group of Seven and returned to the prairies, to Alberta, where he painted and taught for over fifty years. Kerr was director of the art department of the Provincial Institute of Technology and Art for twenty years. He is considered by many to be the most expressive prairie landscape painter ever, and his rhythmic, almost abstract paintings, rich in colour and texture, are in greater demand every year.

☆

**A.C. Leighton** (1901-1965). Leighton was born in England, trained in architecture briefly to please his father, then entered art school. In 1925 he caught the eye of the CPR which employed him to paint advertising posters of the Canadian West: Leighton moved permanently to Calgary in 1929. He founded the Alberta Society of Artists and started a summer school which became the painting department of the Banff School of Fine Arts. A painter of the British watercolour tradition, he painted the light in the Rockies as few others have. The rich tonal variety of his colours and his impressive ability to convey the atmosphere of space and sky in the west make him exceptional.

☆

**Barbara Leighton [Barleigh]** (b.1911). Like her husband, A.C. Leighton, Barbara Leighton was born in England but she studied art in Calgary. She is best known for her block prints which are unique in that they are based on his watercolours. She was able to capture the delicacy of the originals in spite of the printmaking process of using up to twelve different blocks per print.

☆

**Pat McCormick** (b.1947). McCormick was born in the United States of Canadian descent. She came to Canada in 1965 to study at the University of Alberta, stayed, and joined the staff of the Provincial Museum and Archives of Alberta, where she is now curator of Ethnology. A camera has never been far from her side. She is currently assembling a major exhibition in Fort Chipewyan in conjunction with the Fort Chipewyan Bicentennial.

☆

**Harold Wellington McCrea** (1887-1969). McCrea was born in Cobourg, Ontario, and came west to Hanna in 1916 because his brother Herbert had started a newspaper there, the *Hanna Herald*. He had been a successful graphic designer in his youth, then turned to portraiture and paintings with an historic, pastoral theme. McCrea lived in Hanna for only a short time before returning to Ontario.

☆

**Don McVeigh** (b.1951). McVeigh was born in Edmonton and studied art at the University of Alberta (BFA) and at the University of Regina (MFA). A watercolourist of great technical ability, McVeigh takes the familiar themes and everyday objects of European still-life tradition and paints them in a representative, realistic style. Lately he has constructed his own still-life objects—tied bundles of cloth, wood, rolled rugs that seem to be alien yet familiar, European yet Indian—and painted evocative, mysterious "portraits" of them.

☆

**Manwoman (Pat Kemball)** (b.1938). Manwoman was studying architecture at UBC when he had an experience he describes as a dramatic inner awakening. It changed his life. He began to study art to express his visionary experiences, and at 27 he legally changed his name to express the state of unity and wholeness he sought. His innovative paintings, worked in pure bright colours, express a childlike innocence and boundless happiness. Manwoman taught art in Alberta for seven years at NAIT and for three years at the University of Alberta. He now lives in his hometown of Cranbrook, B.C.

☆

**Janet Mitchell** (b.1912). A native of Medicine Hat and a self-taught artist, Mitchell has painted the changing seasons and moods of Alberta landscapes and street scenes for over 50 years. Her paintings are spontaneous, in pure strong colours, with a strong sense of fantasy. In them, symbolic figures and animals float and overlap creating works of great feeling and humour. She was elected to the Royal Canadian Academy in 1978.

☆

**Marion Nicoll** (1909-1985). Nicoll was born and lived most of her life in Calgary except for study periods in New York and Europe. She studied art under the influence of the Group of Seven at the Ontario College of Art and, later in Calgary, with A.C. Leighton. After a summer workshop with Will Barnet, she found herself among the first few abstract painters in Alberta. Her work is characterized by strong, expressive symbolic images, flatly patterned. She was an influential teacher in Calgary and Banff for thirty-four years who believed in teaching discipline and the basics, then giving students creative freedom.

☆

**William Panko** (1892-1948). Panko was born in Tulukow, Austria, and immigrated to Canada in 1911. He came west, to Drumheller, was a farmhand in the summers and a coalminer in the winters, until he contracted tuberculosis in 1937. In the Calgary sanatorium, where he would spend the next ten years, he met Marion Nicoll, then an art therapist. She taught him how to mix watercolours, encouraged him to pursue his own naive style, and brought his work to the attention of other artists. His paintings tell stories of his life in the Drumheller valley.

☆

**W.J. Phillips** (1884-1963). Phillips was an established painter by the time he emigrated to Canada from England in 1913. He painted watercolours in the great 19th century British tradition: virtuoso technique, wonderful colour sensitivity, and love of landscape. In Winnipeg, he began to experiment with etching and went on to colour wood block printmaking. During a brief return to England, he studied with a Japanese print master, Urushibara. In the 1940s Phillips moved to Calgary where he taught at the Provincial Institute of Technology and at the Banff summer sessions, while continuing to produce his renowned watercolours and prints.

☆

**Winold Reiss** (1888-1953). Reiss was born in Karlsruhe, Germany, and was first taught to paint by his father. He later studied at the Royal Academy in Munich. His first visit to the West was in 1919 and he eventually became a naturalized American citizen. Reiss settled in the border country of the Rockies where he ran an art school at St. Mary's Lake in Glacier Park, Montana. He became a friend to the Blackfoot Indians in both Montana and Alberta. They adopted him, naming him Beaver Child. When Reiss died, his Blackfoot friends scattered his ashes in the Rocky Mountain foothills.

☆

**Clifford Robinson** (b.1916). Robinson was born and raised on a ranch in southern Alberta. He was fortunate to study printmaking under W.J. Phillips at the Provincial Institute of Technology and Art in Calgary. Phillips encouraged and actively supported his work. Robinson preferred the linocut to the block print because of its directness and graphic quality. His prints of the 1940s are rich in realistic detail; his later work less so, as in the symbolic and allegorical scenes of Doukhobor life.

☆

**Carl Rungius** (1869-1959). Rungius was born in Germany and moved to America in his twenties. As a child he was keenly interested in drawing wildlife. He became a well-known illustrator for American sportsmen's magazines and travelled to Wyoming, the Yukon, and Alberta. He fell in love with the Rockies and spent the next fifty years of his life painting the animals and mountains around Banff, spending summers in Banff sketching and winters in New York City painting his famous oils.

☆

**Roy Salopree** (b.1953). Salopree is a Treaty Indian artist of the Dene Tha Nation. He was born in Fort Vermilion and began to study art formally at the University of Alberta in 1985, when he won a first prize scholarship. His images stem from his belief that all of nature is connected: sky, land, trees, animals, water, and humans are drawn in relation to the natural world.

☆

**Robert Scott** (b.1941). Meefort, Saskatchewan was the birthplace of this well-known abstract artist. He studied art at the Alberta College of Art in Calgary and received an MFA from the University of Alberta. Scott sculpts paint on the canvas with his hands, achieving a palpable, undulating surface of multilayered colours.

☆

**Orest Semchishen** (b.1932). Semchishen was born in Mundare, Alberta, and is a radiologist in Edmonton. His most well-known work are his 1976 photographs of the Eastern Rite churches of Alberta which culminated in an exhibition at the Edmonton Art Gallery and a book, *Byzantine Churches of Alberta*. As an historical record alone they are of significance. Semchishen's eloquent homage to his heritage has expanded to include other subject matter, but a masterful darkroom technique and sensitivity continue to infuse his work.

☆

**Margaret Shelton** (1915-1984). Shelton was born in Alberta and spent her lifetime interpreting its landscape. She trained initially to be a teacher but later enrolled fulltime at the Provincial Institute of Technology and Art. She was a student of A.C. Leighton, H.G. Glyde, Marion Nicholl and W.J. Phillips. She drew, painted in oils and watercolours, but her excellent draughtsmanship found its métier in block printing. Her finely crafted, direct works have just begun to receive the attention they deserve.

☆

**Wendy Toogood** (b.1947). British born, Toogood came to Canada in 1952, studied at the ACA in Calgary and later in Mexico. Her fabric constructions are hand-stitched and quilted. Fabric is used throughout the design process and is used in the final works in a great variety of textures and densities. To her, colour is fabric rather than paint.

☆

**Sylvain Voyer** (b.1939). Voyer, a native Edmontonian, studied painting and printmaking at the Alberta College of Art in Calgary. Although he has always drawn and painted the landscape, he established his presence in the 1960s with acrylics of severe geometric figures which dealt with space and the illusion of space. His imagery has changed, in recent years, with his growing concerns with the environment, and he has produced highly realistic landscapes and city scenes. While they have expanded in size from miniatures to large compositions, the concerns with spatial problems and the meticulous brushwork remain.

☆

**Joe Weiss** (b.1896). Weiss immigrated to Canada from Switzerland in 1921 and settled in Jasper in 1925 where he began his career as a photographer, and mountaineering guide. He is self-taught but was influenced by Japanese printmaking. Initially, his photos were taken to document expeditions or to show to prospective clients but later became an end in themselves. Weiss was one of the first proponents of ski touring in the Jasper area and has a mountain named after him, Mt. Weiss, in the Winston Churchill range.

☆